'This is *more* than a simple
book for those who desire
well versed in the life and
an immensely able teache   ...... s
imaginative pattern of praying the Bible. The fact that Luther first
introduced his pattern of praying to his hairdresser underlines the
down to earth practical teaching in Luther's writings on prayer. The
"business end" of this book, with the examples of how to use the
Bible in praying, is brilliant and highly commended for use personally
and with small groups.'
David Coffey OBE, Global Ambassador, BMS World Mission

'Michael Parsons proves a wise and gentle guide to reading the word
of God not only with our head but with our hearts. His passion for the
Bible and Luther is infectious.'
Amy Boucher Pye, author of *The Living Cross* (BRF, 2016)

'This superb book offers practical advice for individuals and groups
to experience prayer afresh as a place of encounter with God. Three
excellent chapters outline Luther's scripture-centred approach,
followed by an imaginative series of steps where the author first
allows us to "overhear" how this works for him before we are nudged
to have a go ourselves. This book could change your life!'
David Kerrigan, General Director, BMS World Mission

'Mike Parsons rightly understands that the general dissatisfaction
most Christians feel about the state of their prayer lives often stems
from a tendency to dissociate prayer from Bible reading. Of course,
the two belong together. In this wonderful book, peppered with
fascinating anecdotes and insights from the life of Martin Luther, the
author leads us—via worked examples in scripture—to life-giving
prayer habits. The tone is relaxed and conversational, the content
is theologically rich, and the ideas are eminently practical. So I urge
you: take, read, confess, worship and pray!'
Paul Hedley Jones, Trinity College, Queensland, Australia

'This book is brilliant! It may well be the best book on Luther to appear during these 500 year celebrations—biographical, theological, pastoral and practical. Mike Parsons has done an amazing job of mining and distilling the great reformer's teaching on prayer to help us walk closer with the Lord.'
Simon Ponsonby, Pastor of Theology, St Aldates, Oxford

'Written in a warm and accessible tone, but with a real sense of purpose, this book brings the prayer life of Martin Luther alive for a new generation. I have no doubt that it will change the prayers of all those who read it, as it inspires us to dig deeper into scripture and press further into prayer with warm encouragement and practical examples. A much needed book which effortlessly combines Reformation wisdom with 21st-century warmth. I am excited to see what difference it makes to the prayer life of the church today.'
Nell Goddard, author of *Musings of a Clergy Child* (BRF, 2017)

'This excellent resource takes important Reformation insights, makes them accessible, and then applies them to prayer today. There are many healthy biblical insights here and, if acted upon, they have the potential to enrich our prayer lives greatly. I wish this book a wide readership.'
Peter J. Morden, Vice Principal and Director of the Spurgeon's Centre for Spirituality, Spurgeon's College, London

Praying
the Bible with Luther

A simple approach to everyday prayer

MICHAEL PARSONS

The Bible Reading Fellowship
15 The Chambers, Vineyard
Abingdon OX14 3FE
brf.org.uk

The Bible Reading Fellowship (BRF) is a Registered Charity (233280)

ISBN 978 0 85746 503 0
First published 2017
10 9 8 7 6 5 4 3 2 1 0
All rights reserved

Text © Michael Parsons 2017
This edition © The Bible Reading Fellowship 2017
Cover images © Thinkstock

The author asserts the moral right to be identified as the author of this work

Acknowledgements
Unless otherwise stated, scripture quotations are taken from The Holy Bible, New International Version (Anglicised edition) copyright © 1979, 1984, 2011 by Biblica. Used by permission of Hodder & Stoughton Publishers, an Hachette UK company. All rights reserved. 'NIV' is a registered trademark of Biblica. UK trademark number 1448790.

Scripture taken from *THE MESSAGE*. Copyright © 1993, 1994, 1995, 1996, 2000, 2001, 2002. Used by permission of NavPress Publishing Group.

The New Jerusalem Bible © 1985 by Darton, Longman & Todd Ltd and Doubleday, a division of Bantam Doubleday Dell Publishing Group, Inc.

Every effort has been made to trace and contact copyright owners for material used in this resource. We apologise for any inadvertent omissions or errors, and would ask those concerned to contact us so that full acknowledgement can be made in the future.

A catalogue record for this book is available from the British Library

Printed and bound by CPI Group (UK) Ltd, Croydon CR0 4YY

Contents

Introduction

I should be upfront about this book. It's not a book *about* the reformer, Martin Luther. It isn't a biography of the man and his times, for example; nor a study of his theology. There are quite a few books like that published to commemorate the 500 years since the Lutheran Reformation in Europe (1517), but this isn't one of them. And, it's not a book *about* prayer, either, though there will be a number published on that topic this year too, I've no doubt. So, what is the book about? It's actually a resource book, a practical aid to help readers to pray. It uses a method of praying that Luther employed, so it necessarily introduces him and his method in Chapters 1 and 2 to give some idea of the man and his spirituality—particularly his approach to praying. Chapter 3 adopts his method and applies it to our situation in the 21st century.

What was his method of praying? Briefly, he believed firmly that the words of the Bible and our own praying should be joined together, combined to form a strong, faithful approach to God. He developed a *lectio divina* reading of the Bible from which he prayed. This is a straightforward way of praying that will be explained again and practised through the following chapters.

Luther would begin each dedicated time of prayer with a reading of a scriptural passage. Seeking the Lord's help, he would meditate on it with the following four 'strands' uppermost in his mind. Then he would pray, having his thoughts shaped by his reading:

- instruction, or teaching: What do I need to know?
- thanksgiving, or grateful praise: What should I be grateful for?
- confession, or repentance: What sins shall I confess?
- prayer, or supplication: What do I now need to pray for?

This book is a straightforward resource to help you to pray in a similar fashion: reading scripture, reflecting on what it means to you and praying.

After introducing Martin Luther and his method, the book begins to apply it to praying today. Chapter 4 demonstrates Luther's method in action, beginning by the end of the chapter to ask you to take part. Chapter 5 continues in a similar fashion but asks you to do more in terms of the reflection and the prayer. Chapter 6 suggests passages to read, gives some short clues to approach the text with, and leaves you to get on with it. The final chapter advises other contexts in which this method may be used. So it's an incremental approach to using Luther's method. You're not thrown into the deep end, but you'll eventually get there!

You can see from this brief outline that you'll start as a 'novice' and conclude as an 'expert'. You'll find plenty of instructions and assistance on the journey. So let's start with the reformer, Martin Luther, and then move on to his method of praying.

Chapter 1

Praying with Luther today

Let's begin our conversation with a very important statement, one that underlines everything else in this book—that is, the simple assertion that every one of us has been created to pray. You, me, everyone. And that's because we're made in the image of God, made by a personal, relational God; we've been created to respond to and communicate with him, to be in relationship with him, and praying is a crucial part of that relationship.

Because of this, prayer should be part of our DNA, both as people created by God and, perhaps even more so, as Christians, now recreated through the wonderful, powerful work of the Holy Spirit upon us. Prayer is the basis of our Christian experience of the Lord, individually and communally as church together. I can't imagine that you'd disagree with that. So we need to ask ourselves: why is it also true that if we were asked today about our praying, very few of us would be satisfied with our experience of prayer or with our effort or discipline in this area? I sense that few of us would feel we'd worked it out or that we practised it even to our own satisfaction. We've perfected what we call 'arrow prayers'—prayers uttered in times of trouble or elation; we keep things ticking over, as it were, but deliberate, intentional prayer, prayer that takes time and effort, well, that's a different matter for most of us, isn't it?

One of the reasons for this, it seems to me, is that we so easily and readily divorce prayer from reading scripture—hence the title of this book, *Praying the Bible with Luther*. We'll leave Luther for a moment. Let's briefly look at the rest: the Bible and prayer together.

This is where I find the writing of Eugene Peterson helpful. In a typically stimulating and provocative early book, *Working the Angles:*

The shape of pastoral integrity, Peterson warns us to be slow to pray, not to rush into things thoughtlessly. Although he isn't the only writer to caution us in this way, initially it may surprise us. 'This is not an enterprise to be entered into lightly,' he says of prayer.[1] The reasons he gives are thought-provoking, to say the least, but they boil down to the following: 'All we had counted on was some religious small talk, a little numinous gossip, and we are suddenly involved, without intending it and without having calculated the consequences, in something *eternal*.'[2] 'Religious small talk', 'a little numinous gossip'— careless, light prayer, or prayer without thought—suddenly becomes something far grander and more profound because we are in the presence of the living God. Prayer is dangerous, Peterson says; it is potent, it speaks divine words after God. In powerful images, then, he reminds us of the following:

> When we pray we are using words that bring us into proximity with words that break cedars, shake the wilderness, make oaks whirl, and strip forests bare (Psalm 29:5–9). When we pray we use words that may well leave us quavering, soul-shattered, on our faces… (Isaiah 6:5)[3]

So, lamenting the present state of so much praying (and remember he's talking specifically about pastors and church leaders praying), Peterson asks why it is that 'language used at the height of its powers' is often so stagnant, stale and limp. The answer, he suggests, takes us into the heart of what we are up to in this present book. Prayer is so often stagnant, stale and limp, he says, because 'it has been uprooted from the soil of the word of God'; it lacks both 'rootage and nutrient'.[4]

In this image Peterson makes a very important point. He reminds us that prayer should be rooted in the word of God; it should be fed from the words of scripture; it should find its life in the Bible, in the words God has already spoken, in the divine revelation. I wonder what you think of that comment. Let's look at a few biblical examples to see what he's getting at.

Three obvious biblical examples of praying scripture in this way come to mind (although there are others, of course). In the Old Testament, the prophet Jonah prays from inside the big fish, using ideas and words from the psalms; even the structure of his prayer reminds us of some well-known psalms, such as Psalm 34 and Psalm 118. 'In my distress I called to the Lord,' he says, 'and he answered me. From deep in the realm of the dead I called for help, and you listened to my cry' (Jonah 2:2). Compare this with Psalm 34:4, for example: 'I sought the Lord, and he answered me; he delivered me from all my fears'; and verse 6, 'This poor man called, and the Lord heard him; he saved him out of all his troubles'; and again at verse 17, 'The righteous cry out, and the Lord hears them; he delivers them from all their troubles.' We can imagine that the very repetition of the original psalm embeds the structure and the words into the prophet's mind and gives him faith and hope when all hope appears to be vanishing.

From the New Testament we have two clear illustrations of the same thing, though here the prayers are literally quoted portions of scripture. On the cross, in dying agony, Jesus cries out in prayer, 'My God, my God, why have you forsaken me?'—a direct citation from Psalm 22:1. Later, after Jesus' resurrection, the nascent church, fearful for its own life, meets in an upper room in which the newly released Peter and John explain that the Jewish authorities had them arrested and threatened for speaking and healing in the name of Jesus of Nazareth. The church prays, appropriately using the words of Psalm 2:1–2: 'Why do the nations rage and the peoples plot in vain? The kings of the earth rise up and the rulers band together against the Lord and against his anointed.' In their difficult situation the believers see the fulfilment of these words of scripture and pray them together.

You'll notice above that I use the words 'quoted' and 'appropriately using the words of Psalm 2'. I have to admit that these phrases make the process and the decision to use portions of scripture in praying seem somehow objective, detached and rather academic, as if even in difficult circumstances—inside the fish, the agony of the cross, the threatening of the authorities—we can calmly think through our options and decide what words to use. Of course, we *can* decide when we have all the time in the world. We can sit down, read a passage of scripture and use some of its words and phrases. That in itself is certainly not a bad thing. However, that's not what I'm getting at here. And if we go back to Eugene Peterson's image of our prayers being *rooted* in scripture, we have a more organic view of the situation than this—a view in which reading scripture and praying are closer, unforced, engaged; in which praying the Bible becomes instinctive and a 'living' experience; in which we grow, rooted in scriptural words, speaking them after God.

In the pages that follow, we'll be reading passages of scripture and praying with them. I'm hoping for some development as we progress and become well practised: development from a detached reading-to-prayer to a more organic prayer-rooted-in-scripture. This won't happen overnight, of course, nor will it happen 'accidentally'. It will best occur if we take scripture seriously as the powerful word of the living God to us and if we learn to read it with our heart as well as with our mind. That's why we'll be reading each passage a number of times, not simply once; and why we'll be reflecting on the scripture before launching ourselves into prayer. But more of that in Chapter 3.

Where does Martin Luther fit in?

Martin Luther, the great Protestant reformer, knew all about the connection between God's self-revelation and prayer, between 'dangerous' words spoken and authentic spiritual experience. Let me briefly outline two episodes in his early years that seem to have shaped his Christian experience and his praying, for the rest of his life.

The first happened in 1505 when he was a young man. While walking through dense woods near his home, Luther was unexpectedly caught in a violent thunderstorm. The sky turned opaque and black above him. A sudden and fearsome bolt of lightning, hitting a tree nearby, sent him sprawling and tumbling down a bank, leaving him shaken and afraid. Today, we may think of this experience as 'bad luck' or merely a coincidence; we sometimes use phrases like 'being in the wrong place at the wrong time'. But in Luther's day a bolt of lightning striking that close to someone was not so flippantly brushed aside. To most 16th-century Europeans it was considered to be a sure sign of the displeasure and judgement of God. So here he was, terrified not just by the lightning, which was bad enough, but also by what it signified—the disapproval of almighty God himself. This thunderbolt was none other than God's message revealing something of himself. And he was still in the midst of the terrible storm. Then and there, seemingly without hesitation, he vowed to St Anne (the mother of the Virgin Mary) that, if he was saved from the threatened divine punishment, he would become a monk and devote the rest of his life to God. He was spared and, accordingly, he later entered the Monastery of the Observant Augustinian friars in the German city of Erfurt.

Even if today we don't fully understand this response to the situation, the young Luther's decision at least indicates to us how serious he was about his own salvation and spiritual well-being.

This was the first of two life-changing events in which Luther discerned the revelation of God. Just two years later came the second. After joining the monastery, Luther spent his days in prayer, in singing, in meditation and in peaceful fellowship with the other monks. Days in the monastery were long, starting early in the morning, uninterrupted and largely peaceful. However, this religious routine was shattered when, on 2 May 1507, the young priest, still learning his vocation, was instructed to conduct his first Mass. In the middle of officiating at that eucharistic meal, he experienced something of the majesty and holiness of God—as he had in the thunderstorm—and this he found nothing short of terrifying. In the midst of the Mass he sensed the terror of the Holy, of the Infinite God, and froze, virtually paralysed, unable to proceed. The Prior in charge of the service had to gently persuade him to continue, which he did after a great deal of coaxing and encouragement.

What had happened? In the introductory part of the Mass, Luther had to say of the consecrated elements, lifting up the bread and the wine: 'We offer unto you, the living, the true, the eternal God.' It was at the point of speaking of God as 'living', 'true' and 'eternal', and realising that it was *this* God who was present with them at the altar, that he froze. Can you imagine this? He was tongue-tied, speechless, frightened in front of his contemporaries and superiors. Later in life, Luther reflected on this incident and reported it in typically strong language:

> At these words ['We offer unto you, the living, the true, the eternal God'] I was utterly stupefied and terror-stricken. I thought to myself, 'With what tongue shall I address such Majesty, seeing that all men ought to tremble in the presence of even an earthly prince? Who am I, that I should lift up my eyes or raise my hands to divine Majesty?… At his nod the earth trembles. And shall I, a miserable little pygmy, say, "I want this, I ask for that?" For I am dust and ashes and full of sin and I am speaking to the living, eternal and true God.'[5]

If we remember Eugene Peterson's words about the difference between what we *think* we're doing when we pray and what we are *actually* doing, it might help us here. He said, 'All we had counted on was some religious small talk, a little numinous gossip, and we are suddenly involved, without intending it and without having calculated the consequences, in something *eternal*.'[6] Had Martin Luther supposed that he was involved in 'some religious small talk', as it were, without calculating the magnitude of his actions, through which he was entangled in 'something *eternal*'? It seems likely. But, certainly, it was when he reflected on who God was as God had revealed himself in scripture (majestic, living, eternal, true) that the enormity of prayer before the divine presence struck him.

Martin Luther was a monk for over ten years, and during this time he continued to agonise over that question asked during the Mass. How could someone unworthy, sinful, and unrighteous—which he honestly knew himself to be—stand before the divine majesty? How dare he ask anything of God? How could he, who had transgressed the law in thought, word and deed, confront the divine holiness with a request? His first hymn speaks of this:

I fell but deeper for my strife,
there was no good in all my life,
for sin had all possessed me.
Luther's Works (LW) 53.219

These questions may seem strange and antiquated to many of us today, but they reflect something of the teaching of the church of Luther's childhood. He knew, only too well, about God's holiness and majesty, and this terrified him. What he didn't know in his own experience was God's grace and mercy. Understandably, perhaps, his seeking after this knowledge now became quite desperate.

In God's grace during these formative years, the Lord supplied a godly and caring mentor to counsel him in his ordeal. How often does God do that! Johann von Staupitz became a spiritual father to Luther, advising him to cling to Jesus Christ and to understand God *only through* Jesus Christ as recorded in the Bible. Luther remarked some time later, 'My good Staupitz said, "One must keep one's eyes fixed on that man who is called Christ."'[7]

What finally changed Martin Luther's thinking about God and gave him the release from guilt and anxiety he so longed for? What gave him confidence before this majestic God? What allowed him to pray from his heart, knowing that the Lord heard him and would answer? What allowed him to move from 'religious small talk' to something eternal? The simple answer is that a good and clear reading of scripture did. The reformer lectured through Psalms, Galatians and Hebrews, but it seems to have been his reading and reflection on

Paul's letter to the Romans that made the vital difference. Gradually, he realised that he'd had it all wrong for many years.

Luther's first reading of Romans 1:17, 'For in the gospel the righteousness of God is revealed', seemed only to underline the brutal fact that God is righteous—that is, unapproachable in holiness, unreachable because of who he is. That's what Luther felt was being revealed by the gospel. However, the more he read (and notice his perseverance here), the more he realised that Paul was saying something quite different. The verse continues, 'a righteousness that is by faith from first to last, just as it is written: "The righteous will live by faith".'

Luther started to do the maths, as it were. God is righteous. Yes, he knew that only too well; he'd always known that; he was fully persuaded of it. He never lost or reduced that thought at all; it stayed as a central, core truth of his theology. But he came to see that God reveals that righteousness through the gospel of Jesus Christ, *giving* that righteousness to those who have faith. The verse now made sense. It made evangelical sense; that is, it showed to Luther the good news of the gospel, the evangel, and it centred on the goodness of God in Jesus Christ (*LW* 31.99).

Through this reading he'd found what was, for him, a new view of God. He came to realise that the holy God who terrified him is the all-merciful God, too. The God whose holiness and majesty had made Luther feel totally unworthy had been revealed *in Christ* as a God who deeply loved the world as well. In truth, God is *for us* in Jesus Christ, *not* against us (see Romans 8:31). And he came to realise, too, the central part that Jesus Christ played in all of this: that is, Christ's righteousness was credited or freely given to the person with faith, while that person still remained a sinner. The wonderful image that Luther often employs is of the blanket of Christ's sinlessness draped over the sinner, a blanket that covers or hides our sin. In this, God declares sinners to be what in themselves they are not—that is, righteous before God and able to stand before God. The heart of

Luther's teaching, therefore, is that in Jesus Christ, God has given himself for us, utterly and without reserve. Finally, he'd discovered in scripture a gracious God.

God loves us in Jesus Christ! Martin Luther loved Jesus Christ simply because through him we find access to the living God, through him we have salvation, through him we have life, and through him we have peace and a clear conscience. It's not by accident, nor is it inappropriate, that the Missouri Synod of the Lutheran Church in America has on its website the commemorative statement: 'Reformation 2017. It's *still* all about Jesus.' Staupitz' advice was all about Jesus. Luther's theology is all about Jesus. A biblical view of Jesus Christ reformed the young Luther. It energised him in his own spirituality. It transformed him, releasing him to his life's work—leading the first years of the spiritual revival, which was the 16th-century Reformation.

Martin Luther and us today

So where does all that leave us today? What has it all to do with us as we try to pray? It seems to me that Martin Luther is a really good example of someone who discovered through reading the Bible that God is a good and saving Father, and that he saves through the gracious work of his Son, Jesus Christ. The discovery released Luther into spiritual freedom.[8] Part of this freedom was that it gave him the liberty to pray. It thrust him into the vocation to which the Lord was calling him.

Martin Luther was not perfect, of course. He was very human. In the next chapter we'll be looking briefly at his short book, *How One Should Pray, for Master Peter the Barber*, or *A Simple Way to Pray*, and we'll be seeking to use his method of prayer in later chapters. However, it's important to know something of his journey into faith, because what we've seen here lies at the back of all he says about prayer—that it's a conversation between the faithful believer and their gracious God, that it's fundamentally simple, and that the strength of praying is found in its rootedness in scripture, as Peterson has reminded us more recently.

None of this came easily to the reformer, as we've seen. He had to struggle with his own false beliefs and his own preconceptions of God and misreading of scripture. We may admire his perseverance and his single-mindedness. Perhaps we can find something of that in our own approach to prayer, because when we pray we *are* doing something with eternal consequences. I would suggest that, in a church that can today be light on commitment and fuzzy about its use of language, we are reminded that through spiritual discipline and energy we can re-engage scripture and prayer in a way that stretches our faith and roots our being in divine words and presence.

Where to from here?

I'm not any good at sudoku. I think I'm doing well until I realise, towards the end, that the grid just isn't going to be filled, because I've gone wrong somewhere. But the rest of my family have been experts for some time. I know that some sudoku books begin with 'easy' examples and progressively get more difficult as the sudoku player becomes more competent. (I've never progressed beyond 'easy'!) I've attempted to structure this book around that principle—starting at an easy level, gradually progressing to a more difficult one. How does this work out in practice? Let me explain.

Chapter 4 offers a number of biblical passages that we might use to read and pray through, following Luther's method. They are presented in a straightforward way. On each, I do my own thinking out loud and meditation on the text, followed by prayers in Luther's manner. This will give you a full view of what it means to pray the 'four strands' that Luther speaks of (more of this later). In that sense, it will be 'easy': you merely need to read the chapter, although towards the end I'll be asking you to complete some of the exercises. Chapter 5 repeats the approach, but this time the reading and consideration of the passages will be only partially completed, asking you to complete the task. In other words, it will give you a good start, but won't complete the exercise for you. A little harder! Chapter 6 lists some more biblical texts, asking you to do the whole exercise yourself. In that sense, it will be more 'difficult'. But by the time you reach the end of Chapter 6, you'll feel you have a grasp of the method and hopefully will be eager to move to your own readings at your own pace. The final chapter rounds off the exercises with a short reflection on their benefits.

But first, it would be good to take some time to reflect on the things we've been looking at in this chapter. The following questions may be a good place to start.

- Reflect on Eugene Peterson's words at the beginning of this chapter. Would you agree that prayer is somehow 'dangerous', not to be undertaken lightly? Will this conclusion help or hinder your own praying?
- Our experiences of God will not necessarily be as dramatic as Luther's were, but are you able to reflect on any that have given you a different view of God or of Jesus Christ than the one you previously held?
- Have you had to change your understanding of any biblical theme or passage over the years? Which? Do you remember why this change occurred?
- Take time to reflect on the significance of Jesus Christ to your relationship with God and your ongoing spirituality and prayer.

Chapter 2

A simple way to pray

At one very important level, the 16th-century Protestant Reformation was a pastoral movement. It wasn't simply a period of changing ideas at an intellectual, theoretical or even theological level. These new theological perspectives had a tremendous impact not only on what people believed, but also on the way they behaved, lived their lives and worshipped. As we saw in the previous chapter, the Lutheran Reformation began with a young man desperately seeking a gracious God and his own salvation; it continued as a spiritual revival or renewal in which pastors and teachers used the Bible and spiritual direction to teach others how to find their salvation and to engage with God as Father through Jesus Christ.

In that very personal context, there was no shortage of published works on prayer. Many of the reformers wrote on the subject, and all of them preached on it in their systematic preaching through the books of the Bible. It is interesting to note that despite differences of approach, there were several common emphases in these works, those we might call particularly 'reformational emphases'. They included:

- the sovereignty of the God who answers prayer
- the fatherhood of God to whom we pray
- the importance of faith, hope and certainty in the supplicant
- the central significance of Jesus Christ in God hearing and answering us and his significance to our approach to God
- the pivotal position of the Lord's Prayer for understanding

Naturally, the reformers had different perspectives on the theme of prayer and stressed different things, but on these few key topics they seem to have generally agreed.

In an early work, *An Exposition of the Lord's Prayer for Simple Laymen* (1519), written just two years after his attack on Tetzel's method of selling indulgences, Martin Luther stresses that prayer is a 'spiritual good' and that true and acceptable prayer lifts up both the heart and the mind to God (*LW* 42.124–30). Against the common practice of prayer as mere rote, Luther asserts that prayer from the heart is an inner longing, a sighing or a desiring. So, what comes across strongly in Luther's early teaching on prayer is that it is, at its core, relational. It has to do with the relationship between the supplicant and their God, one of a child approaching their Father. We'd expect that from a young man who had only recently discovered that God was for him, not against him, wouldn't we? And so, understandably, he stresses that in prayer the believer needs to move God to mercy, while all the time putting our confidence in the fact that the sovereign, holy God is actually our gracious Father—a word which he says is 'a friendly, sweet, intimate, and warm-hearted word' (*LW* 42.22).

A few years later, in 1528, we find the reformer again expounding the fatherhood of God as the foundation for understanding and, more importantly, practising prayer. In a sermon preached in that year, he uses the wonderful metaphor of a sack that the faithful hold open before their Father, in which we receive more and more, the longer we hold it open, for the Lord in his mercy desires or even longs to give (*LW* 51.171). Another important emphasis is added in this work. Luther speaks of true prayer as obedience. He states this emphatically: 'You should pray and you should know that you are bound to pray by divine command.' Again he spells it out, 'This work [that is, prayer] I have been commanded to do and as an obedient person I must do it' (*LW* 51.170). This isn't something we tend to stress today (perhaps we should), but it became an important element in the Reformation. In fact, Luther attaches the spiritual exercise of prayer firmly to the second commandment. Expounding that commandment, he insists that believers must not use the Lord's name in vain, but that this conversely, in itself, *requires* us to use God's name in worship and adoration. That is the positive corollary to the negative commandment concerning the wrongful use of the Lord's name.

We might at first find this rather strange. We sometimes want prayer to be spontaneous and relational, not directed by law and rules. However, Luther speaks of obedience to the law as demonstrating our relationship with God. We are obedient because God loves us and we respond to that love. This, then, he says, gives added confidence to those of us who would call on the name of the Lord. Luther states that as God has demanded prayer from us, so he will graciously answer our obedient petitions. In typically forthright manner, at times he insists that God is therefore *bound* to answer his children, saying at one point that if Judas Iscariot himself had prayed for forgiveness, the Lord would have granted it, such is his commitment to answering heartfelt prayer.

Early in 1535 Luther wrote an open letter, *How One Should Pray, for Master Peter the Barber*, or *A Simple Way to Pray*. Master Peter Beskendorf was Luther's hairdresser and had apparently been talking to him about how difficult he found it to pray as he should, asking the reformer for his advice on how best to proceed. It is noteworthy that in the midst of a mountain of work that would sink most mortals—lecturing, preaching, writing significant Reformation works, letter writing, pastoral commitment, political engagement, church leadership and a great deal besides—Luther found time to write a practical short work for his barber on how to pray. Of course, very little of what the reformer did remained so singularly focused, and that is true of this work, too. He wrote with others in mind, such was his pastoral perspective and the importance that he attached to believers praying.

Before looking briefly at the work, we might notice, perhaps, the unfortunate conclusion to Luther's and his barber's relationship. Shortly after Luther had written the work, Master Peter got drunk and stabbed his own son-in-law to death. His son-in-law had claimed, presumably while also very drunk, that no one could harm him—that he was somehow indestructible. Evidently he wasn't! Peter was charged with murder and faced the death sentence, until his friend Martin Luther stepped in and managed to get the sentence commuted to banishment for life from the city of Wittenberg. As far as is known, that was the end of their relationship.

Luther's short work on prayer

So, let's take a brief look at Luther's thoughts on prayer from this short piece for his hairdresser. It's here that he outlines a method of prayer that we can follow and gain spiritual direction from, even today.[9] We'll take a brief look at Luther's advice more generally before focusing on the method he outlines, the method that we'll be practising in the rest of this book, from Chapter 3 onwards.

Luther's own experience of prayer

The first thing we notice about this work is that Luther speaks from his own experience of prayer. He is not embarrassed at opening up and being suitably vulnerable with his readers. This is a very human characteristic of Luther. Unlike some other reformers, notably the more reticent John Calvin, he often uses his own life experience to teach others, knowing that those to whom he writes will be going through the same failures and successes as he experiences. The opening sentence suggests this: 'I will tell you as best I can what I do personally when I pray.' He is empathetic as well. He confesses that at times he, too, becomes 'cool and joyless' in prayer—blaming both his own flesh and the devil for that obstruction to prayer.

It is, of course, quite heartening to know that the great German reformer found himself 'cool and joyless' in prayer, but it is not something that should encourage us to complacency. When he finds himself in this state, he says that he either enters a room on his own to read and to pray, or, if the time is appropriate, goes into the church 'where a congregation is assembled' to do the same. In this way, he either finds a quiet place in solitude (see Matthew 6:6) or finds fellow believers with whom to seek the Lord (see Hebrews 10:25). Notice, though, that by saying this he encourages us to do something about the problem immediately. There is a danger of neglect if we procrastinate at this point.

The practice of prayer

The second thing that is immediately noticeable is the practical nature of the writing. This short work is not a theoretical thesis or an exegetical commentary on prayer, but a work on *how to pray*. It's not so much about the nature of prayer, but about its practice. Indeed, even in the busyness and complexity of the Reformation, Luther remained serious about his pastoral calling, and to help people to pray was an integral part of that vocation. So, for example, he advises us not to delay our praying by thinking that after we've done something else we will return to prayer. He knows as well as we do, perhaps, that we probably will not return to pray and then, he laments, 'nothing comes of prayer that day'. Even though he shows some appreciation of the thought that everything we do in faith is prayer,[10] he advises us 'not to break the habit of true prayer', by which he means those times of intentional fellowship with God our Father, times of determined, focused prayer and worship. Our flesh, he says, is naturally 'disinclined to the spirit of prayer' and if we consider everything to be prayer, then in the end nothing will be prayer. We will become lazy, doing nothing and praying nothing.

Luther links the reciting of scripture, Jesus' words, the ten commandments and so on with praying briefly—kneeling or standing, 'with your hands folded and your eyes toward heaven'. The connection between reciting scripture and praying is extremely important (as underlined in the Introduction) and we will pick it up again in Chapter 3. Luther's short work specifically singles out the Lord's Prayer, the ten commandments and the creed as appropriate texts to recite before prayer, texts which he insists should warm our hearts and encourage us to pray. Later, he widens this encouragement to include any text of scripture that does the same. The words and truths of scripture will persuade our hearts to be turned towards speaking with God in prayer, particularly as they direct us to the person of Jesus Christ—again, something else we'll look at in Chapter 3 and beyond.

The reformer's section on the Lord's Prayer allows us to see this in practice. Here he takes each petition, recites and repeats it, and prays through its implications both for himself and for the world around him. For instance, he takes the first petition, 'Hallowed be your name'. He reads the petition in the context of the whole prayer, then repeats and recites it aloud until it has sunk deep into his heart and thinking. At that point he is ready to pray through it and with it. He asks the Lord to root out all error and false teaching which, he says, blasphemes and dishonours the Lord's name. This is understandable, given his immediate context, a context in which he is seeking to reform the church. Then he asks that God might convert those who don't yet know him, or, if they resist him, at least restrain them from disrespecting God's own name.

The shape of the whole exercise noticeably takes into account both the wider world around Luther and his immediate circumstances. Much of what he says relates to the troubled, violent and confusing world in which he lived; but much relates to his own spiritual well-being and that of his family and friends. For example, in responding to the fourth petition, 'Give us this day our daily bread', the reformer prays for peace and protection, for the Emperor's welfare, for his prince and his subjects, for people in towns and those on the outlying farms, about the weather and for a good harvest. Lastly, he commends his own household—'property, wife and child'—to the Lord. Interestingly, under what he calls 'temporal and physical life', he prays for protection against the devil and his fallen angels. So, the shape and the reach of his praying are remarkably universal, not simply concentrated on his own narrow, though admittedly important, needs.

What other practical things does the reformer say? He speaks of confidence—always an important feature of Luther's theology. Note what he states at the end of his section on the Lord's Prayer, for example. 'Finally,' Luther says, 'mark this, that you must always speak the Amen firmly.' This affirmation shows our confidence in God—not only that he has heard our prayer, but also that he has said 'Yes!' to it. When we pray, Luther insists, we should do so knowing that we stand with 'all devout Christians', with the whole of the church (see Hebrews 12:1), united in prayer before God's throne. Luther's conclusion is that God cannot disdain our prayers, for 'That is what Amen means.'

The reformer is also clear that he doesn't want every day's prayer to be identical to that of every other day; he doesn't want us to get into a repetitive rut in our praying. He prefers that our hearts be stirred by what we read, that our thoughts be guided by what we've recited and thought through. 'I say my prayers in one fashion today, in another tomorrow, depending upon my mood and feeling,' he admits. So, he encourages us to be flexible, lest we fall into a lazy habit of always saying the same things, in which there is no room for the Holy Spirit to teach us. In fact, it seems to me that the exceptional element in this particular work—and one worth contemplating in our own prayer lives—is that the reformer refuses to be tied to rules and what we might call a bland 'normality'. Noticeably, he allows space for a genuine, intimate experience of the Holy Spirit working through the word of God. He says:

> If in the midst of such thoughts [on reading the Lord's Prayer] the Holy Spirit begins to preach in your heart with rich, enlightening thoughts, honour him by *letting go of this written scheme*: be still and listen to him who can do better than you can. Remember what he says and note it well and you will behold wondrous things in the law of God.
>
> LW 43.201–202, emphasis added

Therefore, perhaps with an eye to Paul's words in Romans 8:26–27[11] and certainly in the context of his own thoroughly relational theology, Luther moves and directs us away from an empty and idolatrous rote and towards an experiential piety in which God himself may be the prime mover.

Luther calls for an eagerness and a readiness in prayer. He speaks, too, of attentiveness, appropriately using the illustration of a barber who would get into trouble if he lost concentration while shaving someone. He could cut a nose, a mouth, or even a throat, he says. 'Thus, if anything is to be done well,' the reformer concludes, 'it requires the full attention of all one's senses and members.'

A garland of four strands

This brings us to a description of the method of prayer that we're going to practise in the chapters that follow—what the reformer calls a *garland of four strands*. He suggests that if he has time, he takes each commandment, one after another, and divides it into four parts, 'thereby fashioning a garland of four strands'. He then consciously considers each strand as a different aspect of his reading/praying. First comes instruction ('which is what it is intended to be,' he says). At this point, the question he asks himself is simply, what the Lord demands of him 'so earnestly'. Then he turns his consideration of the commandment to thanksgiving, then confession and, lastly, to prayer or supplication.

Later, he speaks of this as a commandment's 'fourfold aspect', perhaps here implying the strength of the aspects together, like a rope made from four cords intertwined for a single greater strength. Later still, towards the conclusion of this section, Luther uses another helpful metaphor, speaking of these same aspects as a school book, a song book, a penitential book and a prayer book, respectively. So, the four strands or aspects are as follows:

- instruction, or teaching (a school book)
- thanksgiving, or grateful praise (a song book)
- confession, or repentance (a penitential book)
- prayer, or supplication (a prayer book)

These help to shape Luther's contemplation of the text and enable him to pray in a more biblically engaged way. A brief look at how this is accomplished will suffice to show what he intends.[12] He starts by reading or reciting the first commandment, 'You shall have no other gods before me', to himself out loud. The four strands of instruction, thanksgiving, confession and supplication follow; but what we need to notice is the thought or meditation that has gone on between reciting the commandment and the strands. His repeated reading of the commandment encourages him to think through the implications in each strand. This is clear from what he prays.

First, under 'instruction' he suggests that in this commandment, God, declaring himself to be *his* God, expects Luther to trust him alone in everything: for Luther, that is part and parcel of what it is to be a Christian. Second, under 'thanksgiving', the reformer is grateful to God who 'unasked, unbidden and unmerited' has offered to be *his* God. We have sought after all sorts of other things to trust in, he admits, but the Lord, in remarkable and unmerited grace, has told us that he intends to be our God. 'How could we ever in all eternity thank him enough!' Luther rejoices. Third, he confesses having provoked God by his idolatries: 'I repent of these and ask for his grace.' Last, he prays that God would give him understanding of the commandments and the ability to live by them confidently. In this way we see that prayer allows God the initiative in our lives. Luther shapes his response to each commandment in the same way: instruction, thanksgiving, confession and prayer. We'll return to this below, and again in the next chapter.

Interestingly, immediately after his prayers on the sixth commandment and before he begins the seventh, Luther gives the following advice. He says that he continues with the other commandments (seven to ten) 'as I have time for or opportunity or am in the mood for'. As we have already noticed, he is clearly not bound to set form or length of time. In fact, he insists that no one should feel bound by what he says, that he is merely offering an example for anyone wishing to follow. Indeed, he challenges those who feel they might improve on what he's said to do so.

His advice abounds. The commandments, he says, are there to help our heart to grow zealous in prayer. Take care not to grow weary, he says. A good prayer should be short, frequent and earnest. He acknowledges that he hasn't had opportunity to speak about the scriptures' use in prayer, or the psalms' use, but encourages us to 'use them as flint and steel to kindle a flame in the heart'. Hopefully, we'll do just this from Chapter 4 onwards.

Characteristics of Luther's praying

So what are some of the important lessons that we can learn and apply from this short work by Luther on prayer? Here is a simple list of advice from what we've discovered above, roughly in the order in which we noted the points earlier.

- It is common to have periods of disinterest in prayer, but try to resist them.
- Don't delay prayer; don't procrastinate.
- Pray intentionally in a focused manner.
- Recite scripture to encourage prayer and to warm our hearts towards God.
- Pray for the world as well as ourselves and our own circumstances.
- Be confident that the Lord has heard our prayers.
- Know that the context of our praying is as wide as the universal and eternal church itself.
- Be flexible in the structure or shape of our praying.
- Allow space for the inspiring work of the Holy Spirit.
- Be eager to pray.
- Be ready to pray.
- Be earnest, serious and reverent in prayer.
- Pray frequently.

Of course, we might add to this list that in order to shape prayer, we should deliberately read each biblical passage with four aspects in mind: instruction, thanksgiving, confession and supplication.

It's clear that this short list doesn't exhaust everything that Luther says about prayer. He comments, for example, 'It is a good thing to let prayer be the first business of the morning and the last at night', demonstrating its necessity and importance in our day-to-day living before God. Two other characteristics that are evident in Luther's writing are the simplicity of prayer and his sheer enthusiasm for it. Although he seeks to teach a new way of prayer, he keeps his instructions simple and straightforward because prayer itself is a simple way of speaking to God—hence, the enthusiasm. Who would not want to speak with their Father?

This brings us to the very significant underlying matter of our relationship with God in prayer. Luther clearly envisages God as holy, righteous, 'high and exalted' (see Isaiah 6:1); one who demands our prayer and praise; one before whom we stand or kneel, but with our 'eyes towards heaven'—humbled, attentive, waiting, expectant. What comes across from Luther's comments is also that this God is 'for us' (*pro nobis*—a favourite and often repeated phrase in the reformer's writings). God's favour has been gained through Jesus Christ and is a matter of undeserved grace and love. In Christ we already have everything. He alone is the basis on which we approach such a God. This divine favour is recognised in the context of prayer specifically because he speaks to us by his Holy Spirit working through the text of scripture. He is approachable, he listens to us and he answers our petitions with immeasurable generosity and care.

On the other side of the relationship, Luther is clear that we are sinners who would be far removed from God but for the person and the generous redeeming work of Jesus Christ. Our knowledge and experience of this prompt in us gratitude, joy and confidence, together with a profound humility. In his comments on the sixth petition of the Lord's Prayer, 'Lead us not into temptation', he asks, 'O dear Lord, God and Father, keep us fit and alert, eager and diligent in your word and service, so that we do not become complacent, lazy and slothful as though we had already achieved everything.' Though the reformer defines the Christian as simultaneously justified and sinful, he recognises that in Christ we are being sanctified by the Holy Spirit. Yet it's important to remember that we have not 'already achieved everything'.

Luther's prayer from the introduction of the section on the Lord's Prayer collects much of what we've seen so far in Chapters 1 and 2. It's worth quoting this here, and pondering it before we start trying out Luther's method of prayer in Chapter 3 onwards. Here he says the following:

> O heavenly Father, dear God, I am a poor unworthy sinner. I do not deserve to raise my eyes or hands toward you or to pray. But because you have commanded us all to pray and have promised to hear us and through your dear Son Jesus Christ have taught us both how and what to pray, I come to you in obedience to your word, trusting in your gracious promise. I pray in the name of my Lord Jesus Christ together with all your saints and Christians on earth as he has taught us.
>
> LW 43.194

Can you see many of the topics we've been discussing in this single prayer: the humbled, sinful supplicant being obedient to the command of God to pray, trusting and resting in the divine promise; Jesus Christ, the only way to God; a holy God who both commands prayer and promises to hear and to answer it; the importance of the word and the universal context in which we pray?

Reflection

We might reflect on our own praying in light of what Luther says. Why not take time to reflect on the following before moving on to the next chapter?

- How important has prayer been in your Christian life—your own prayer and that of other people?
- Look again at the bulleted list of advice. Take time to consider each aspect in relation to your own praying.
- How do you view your relationship with God and his with you? How are they reflected in your praying?
- How might you allow more openness to the Holy Spirit in your times of prayer? What do you think that might look like?
- How important is it for you to pray with others? How does it add to your experience?

Chapter 3

Praying the Bible today

This chapter brings us to the heart of the book, the 'business end' of what we're about, which is the practice today of Martin Luther's method of praying. This is summarised, as we've seen, in his short treatise on prayer, offered originally to his hairdresser, Peter Beskendorf, and through him to other reforming Christians eager to pray in a way that would be most in line with the new evangelical teaching they were hearing. I've outlined the reformer's helpful and very practical ideas in Chapter 2; and we'll keep these in mind as we come now to pray as Luther advises. It will be useful, too, to remember his theology or teaching, some of which was sketched briefly in Chapter 1. After all, of course, this theology informs his Christian practice or piety. His reformational teaching was never abstract or speculative theology, never divorced from the lived reality of men and women's lives, including and most importantly in their relationship with God.

Luther is offering a form of *lectio divina*, or 'godly reading'. In short, *lectio divina* refers to a prayerful reading of a scripture passage with openness to and expectancy of hearing God speaking through it. As you can see, the definition itself singles out three important elements of this exercise: reading scripture, praying, and being open to the work of the Holy Spirit both through the reading and in response to the prayer.

It's worth remembering that the reformer is adamant that we don't simply repeat what he does in his treatise, but that we broadly follow his example and pray in a similar way. One of the characteristics we have noted in Luther is his desire for flexibility and the ability to change. I'm not suggesting that what follows is exactly what Luther intended; but it is certainly in the spirit of Luther. What follows is an adaptation of his method for a different world, for Christians with access to multiple copies of the Bible (both hard copy and digital) in our own language, for instance;[13] and, importantly, for those living after the Reformation, who have imbibed its ideas and its dynamic, even if unconsciously.

Let's remind ourselves what we're aiming at as we come to pray in this manner. Simply put, we're aiming, by God's grace, to turn a thoughtful reading of scripture into focused, heartfelt prayer. We have noted that one of the metaphors that Luther employs is of a garland of four strands, intended to aid the shape and content of our praying. Each strand is as important as the next, but the order *is* significant. So we meditate on the passage, or parts of it, with the following four aspects or 'strands' uppermost in our minds, seeking the Lord's help:

- instruction, or teaching
- thanksgiving, or grateful praise
- confession, or repentance
- prayer, or supplication

It's important that we see this short list as applying directly to ourselves. Perhaps we can help to ensure that by turning the various strands or aspects into pointed questions—something like the following:

- Instruction, or teaching: What is the Lord seeking to teach me from this passage? What do I need to know?
- Thanksgiving, or grateful praise: What should I be grateful for on reading this portion of scripture?
- Confession, or repentance: How does this passage impinge on my conscience and what in it encourages me to confess particular sins? What sins shall I confess?
- Prayer, or supplication: What do I now need to pray for, to cry out to God for?

As we saw in the previous chapter, this focus on us is not intended to centre all things on ourselves in an egocentric way, as if we are the most important element in this spiritual exchange. Sadly, this may today be the case in many quarters of the church, but it was never the reformer's intention in his own day. Rather, a focus on ourselves helps to ensure the intimate and relational link that Luther wishes to build between the reader, the word of God and God himself. More than that, it is important for us to realise God beyond the Bible, as it were, to experience him through the word, to relate in a personal way to the God with whom we have to do, in whom 'we live and move and have our being,' as the apostle Paul puts it (Acts 17:28). That was foundational to Luther's own spiritual experience.

As we've seen, Luther is convinced that the Lord, the Holy Spirit, 'preaches' to us through the written word of the Bible 'with rich, enlightening thoughts' (*LW* 43.201–202). It is the experiential aspect of this that will inspire, quicken, strengthen and transform us as we read. And we long to experience God in our praying. See Psalm 42:1, for example, where the psalmist longs for God as the deer pants for clean, pure water in a dry, barren, parched landscape. That's a picture that we might like to keep in mind.

So, what do we do? How do we go about it? Here are some guidelines that I've found helpful. These are definitely not rules, merely suggestions gleaned from Luther's writing and my own experience.

On my own or in a group?

The first question to ask ourselves is whether we want to do this exercise on our own or in a small group. I've managed to do both quite successfully. I taught theology for some years at Vose Seminary in Perth, Western Australia. I looked forward to Wednesday morning each week during term as on that day we committed ourselves more intentionally to the devotional and practical life of the students, many of whom were working towards significant ministry of some kind. We worshipped together, had classes for preaching, and so on, and a small fellowship group met for an hour before we ate together, enjoying the chatter of friendship and united purpose. It was in this small group context that I first encountered Luther's teaching on prayer in practice—and it worked beautifully. Each week for a semester we would select a biblical passage, discuss it as a group, consider it together and pray through it as Luther suggests. The advantages were clear. In gleaning each other's different perspectives on scripture and various life experiences, we learned how the Lord uses his word to speak with different people in different circumstances (often from different parts of the world: the US, Russia, China, Korea, Malaysia, the UK, and Australia were all represented) and we often came to new insights and fresh application. It was a privilege and an exciting spiritual discipline to reflect together in that way.

If you're thinking of working with others, it would be a good thing to consider what group you might do these exercises with. It might be advantageous for a church leadership team, for example, to come together seeking direction and wisdom from the Lord at a particular time in the church's life, ministry and mission. Those involved in preaching might use this method in preparation for a series of sermons. Home groups could certainly profit from the use of Luther's four-stranded garland method of praying. Families, friends together, ecumenical groups, Lent and Advent groups, students—whatever the group, members could select passages or a biblical book that might speak to them in their situation and pray through them over the weeks, in a disciplined and persistent way, to find the mind of Christ.

As I say, over many years I've also used this way of prayerful reading quietly on my own and to good effect. Having flagged the possibility of group participation, therefore, the following exercises will presume a single participant seeking the face of God in prayer.

What biblical passages to use

The selection of a biblical passage is crucial to the whole exercise, of course. You might choose a favourite passage or any text that speaks to your present condition; or go through a book in the Bible, section by section; or you may follow a lectionary. Though I would say that the advantages outweigh the disadvantages, reading through a whole biblical book in this way can be a problem, particularly when you're just starting to work it all out. A whole book will usually confront you with subjects and themes you might not have chosen, but it will encourage you to think and pray through what used to be termed 'the whole counsel of God' (see Acts 20:27) in a more comprehensive way than you might have done otherwise. However, I would suggest that you start with passages that you know, perhaps your favourite ones, and work up to a whole book. In any case, make sure that the passage is relatively short (no more than 12 or 13 verses, and ideally considerably less), that it is evidently complete in itself, and that it makes sense as it stands.

Where to sit

It is best to sit in a comfortable chair, in a quiet undisturbed room, where you can concentrate for a period of time. Each exercise may take up to half an hour, but be prepared to lengthen the time if the Holy Spirit begins to 'preach' to you. For this reason alone, personally, I wouldn't use this method every day. Luther suggests flexibility, as we've noted above. It might be good to concentrate on it for a time and then revert to your normal way of praying or 'quiet time'. It might be advisable to use it once or twice a week, perhaps, or on pilgrimage or during a retreat, for the length of a school term, or even on holiday.

Pray for God to help

It's important, I think, to begin each session with a short prayer asking the Lord to be present with you in the exercise; that he will help you understand and grasp the reading, that he might inspire you to respond in ways appropriate for your circumstances. Ask him to speak through the biblical passage, to apply it by his Holy Spirit to you in a very specific and incontrovertible way. Ask that you might know his presence, to conform you more and more into the likeness of his Son, Jesus Christ. In this way we acknowledge our dependence on the Lord, for without his grace working in us we remain weak and wanting.

The reading

Once you're on your own and you've chosen a suitable reading, read it slowly several times, pausing between each time. It's often best to read the passage out loud to yourself (if that's possible), being alert to words or phrases, ideas and repetitions, images, characters and story, allowing the words to sink in. Perhaps stop at words or phrases that specifically speak to you or your situation. Slowly mull them over. You can attempt to read the Bible from the heart as well as from the head, feasting on God's goodness and love.

We all know that today the pace of life seems to get faster and faster. Our 'free' time seems to be less and less. In a perceptive comment, Mark Bradford laments this: 'As the pace of life becomes faster and faster, there is barely enough time to do, let alone to think, reflect and consider whether we are walking the right way.'[14] That's true! Nevertheless, it's important to slow down intentionally, to allow scripture to speak to us words of teaching, comfort, rebuke, correction, encouragement, empowering, peace, freedom and mission. It's important for us to remember, too, that the Bible is a book that both informs and forms us. It informs our minds and our thinking; it forms our beliefs, our faith and our living. So, take time to meditate and to consider. Be still for a while and let God do his transforming work. Ponder each of Luther's four strands before working them out in prayer.

Thinking out loud

Have a sort of brainstorming session. It might mean simply thinking aloud about the content of the biblical passage: what are the main themes, who are the main characters, are there any comparisons being made, and what is it telling me to believe and to do? Also, it's well worth considering whether the passage or specific things in the passage remind you of anything—a biblical text or a past experience. These could be very useful for interpreting what the Lord is saying to you through the text.

Stick to the task in hand

It's absolutely essential to stick to the task in hand. When you've chosen a suitable passage, keep to it, even though all sorts of distractions will try to force themselves upon you. For instance, if you're reading a biblical passage that includes a word you'd love to explore, don't be tempted! Words like 'predestination', 'law', 'freedom', 'covenant' and so on are important words, packed with theology, biblical history and implication. We might be tempted to explore them through commentaries, concordances and the like, but now is not the time. It is important to underline this before we start.

Let me give you an illustration that might help to reinforce this point. You may recall Holman Hunt, the English artist. He painted that beautiful picture of Jesus standing at a door with a brightly glowing lantern in his left hand, knocking to come in. It's often pointed out that the door is lacking a handle, and the reason given is that those inside need to hear Jesus and to answer the door for him; he won't push his way in. One day, Holman Hunt was taking an art class with several students and, looking out of the window, he noticed a most beautiful sunset. His reaction was instant. He told his students to stop what they were doing, to gather their belongings—easels, pencils, colours, brushes and so on—and to rush outside, where they were to paint that sunset. Moments later, walking around encouraging his students, he came to the last one, who was busy with something else. This student had noticed that across the meadow, towards the dying, glorious red sun, was a barn—and the student was drawing the barn. Holman Hunt stood, looked, and said the following: 'You can draw the barn if you like, but the barn will be there tomorrow. Paint the sunset while it's still here!'

I sometimes use this illustration in sermons. If, for example, I'm preaching on freedom, I know that one or two (and more) in the congregation will be thinking about how law fits in—that's human nature, I suppose. So I tell them this illustration to indicate that the distracting word or idea, like the barn, will still be there tomorrow (and the day after, for that matter), so let's focus on what we have today. The same is true of our reading in these exercises. Focus on what you have today. Don't become distracted. If necessary, write down the distracting word or idea and follow it up later.

Take the questions above seriously

It is essential to take the strands seriously and, in order to do that, to ask the suggested questions (along with others) seriously and with an openness of heart and life. When you turn to a passage that includes obvious teaching, look at the obvious and rejoice in it. After all, the exercises are not about thinking new thoughts as much as about thinking God's thoughts after him, as far as we can. For instance, if you read Deuteronomy 6:4, 'Hear, O Israel: the Lord our God, the Lord is one', rejoice in the oneness of God. That's an amazing truth. There is only one God. But we might notice, too, that he also says he is *our* God, and that's something to take pleasure in.

At the point of answering the question about our conscience and confession of sin, take it seriously. Mark Bradford speaks of our society as 'a post-sin society'[15] because there is little consciousness of sin or wrongdoing in it. Sadly, that is self-evidently the case. However, when the God who sees everything about us reminds us through scripture that we are sinners, and that we have sins to confess, let's be countercultural and take it seriously: in repentance is forgiveness and a fresh beginning.

Keep God and Jesus central

Martin Luther stated—because he knew through his own experience—that God is for us, not against us. The apostle Paul declares it in Romans 8:31: 'If God is for us, who can be against us?' It's important to keep that in mind. The overriding teaching of scripture is of the wonderful salvation granted to fallen human beings by the grace of God through Jesus Christ. The Lord is central to that narrative—not Israel, not the church, not us, but God. It helps tremendously if we keep that in mind as we read scripture. This works itself out if, generally, we look at what can be learned first about God, then about ourselves.

This is also the case in relation to the Lord Jesus. We ask what the passage teaches about him, about his ways and his grace; then what it teaches about us. In a group exercise in which I was recently involved, we were asked to pick out the significant words in Galatians 3:13–14, which reads as follows:

> Christ redeemed us from the curse of the law by becoming a curse for us, for it is written: 'Cursed is everyone who is hung on a pole.' He redeemed us in order that the blessing given to Abraham might come to the Gentiles through Christ Jesus, so that by faith we might receive the promise of the Spirit.

Words underlined by the members of the group included 'blessing', 'faith', 'receive' and 'promise', but not 'Christ Jesus'. I wasn't surprised, then, that the ensuing conversation was directed towards *our* task in receiving what was offered—strangely, in the context of Galatians, the very opposite of what the apostle was seeking to stress. Jesus Christ is central!

Whole movements have been birthed as a result of rediscovering this important biblical emphasis—including the Reformation, the Wesleyan Revival, the Great Awakening and others. As we saw in Chapter 1, it was a central and foundational teaching of the Protestant Reformation and of Luther in particular. As a further illustration, consider the narrative of Jesus and Peter walking on the water, found in Matthew 14:22–33. Is the story about Peter or about Jesus? It seems to me that too many contemporary sermons suggest that it's about Peter. 'Step out of the boat' is a fairly typical title. But Luther would insist that the story is about the master, not the disciple; so that sort of title sidesteps the real intention. What does it teach about Jesus? Then, what can we learn about ourselves through Peter's example? Therefore, keep God and Jesus central, not self.

After reading and prayer, wait

Try not to rush away from your time of reading and reflection. Rather, stay put for a while in silence and wait for the Lord to continue to speak. I remember, when I was young, being greatly impressed reading about George Müller, a Prussian by birth, a Christian evangelist and Director of the Ashley Down orphanage in Bristol. He is said to have cared for more than 10,000 orphans during his long life, a life that covered nearly the whole of the 19th century (1805–98). I remember reading of Müller that he would kneel by his bed, read a portion of scripture, pray and then simply wait. He once stated that his habit was to wait on his knees until the Lord spoke to him, and that he would not rise until he had heard from God. That demonstrates faith in a God who speaks. So, if you can, rest in the knowledge that he wants to bless your ways, and wait for him to intimate his grace to you for the days ahead.

Chapter 4

Following Luther's example: starting out

Having outlined Luther's method of praying at some length, perhaps we're ready to make that first attempt at following his example. The first half of this chapter presents some Old Testament passages, the second moves on to New Testament extracts, six of each. These have been carefully selected because they appear to give clear boundaries in terms of their subject. What I mean by that is that each passage appears to come to its own completion; there is no sense of having to wait for the next instalment or the sequel.

The biblical passages are drawn from different genres of scripture— history, poetry, prophecy, Gospel and letter—and will probably elicit very different responses from their readers; that is, from us! They are also well-known passages that most of us will have heard preached, will have read in home groups, and among our family and friends. Like most learning, it's probably easiest to start with what's familiar!

This chapter sees me following Luther's method in order to demonstrate the approach and, hopefully, to draw from a reading of the biblical passages ways of forming our prayers through reflection on God's word. By that, I mean that I have sat down with each of the biblical passages that follow and attempted the reformer's simple way of praying: exploring and thinking through the passage, asking the questions of it and turning what I've discovered into prayer. Essentially, that's what Luther was wanting: thoughtful, heartfelt praying that begins with God (in his word) and ends with God (in worship and gratitude). Before we begin, though, we might just remind ourselves of a couple of things from the preceding chapter.

First, it would be good to remember the four strands that form the method of Bible reading. They are:

- instruction, or teaching
- thanksgiving, or grateful praise
- confession, or repentance
- prayer, or supplication

Then, it will be helpful to keep in mind the questions that will allow and encourage us to apply these aspects to our own lives and spiritual development as followers of Jesus Christ. So we might ask:

- What is the Lord seeking to teach me from this passage? What do I need to know?
- What should I be grateful for on reading this portion of scripture?
- How does this passage impinge on my conscience and what in it encourages me to confess particular sins? What sins shall I confess?
- What do I now need to pray for, to cry out to God for?

Also, here is a reminder of the more pertinent items from the list of guidelines to help make your experience of praying more purposeful.

- Sit in a comfortable chair
- Pray for God to help
- Stick to the task in hand
- Take the suggested questions seriously
- Keep God and Jesus as central, not self
- After reading and prayer, wait

Let me underline before we begin, though, that your reading (that is, your 'thinking out loud') will be different than mine. We are different people with different experiences of life, of church and of God. So don't worry that you might have brought out different things from the biblical passages than I have. Some things will be the same or similar, of course—what we might call the core ideas, perhaps—but others will be our own personal tangents as the Lord speaks to us through the word by his Holy Spirit. That's the way it works! And you'll notice too that the passages are of different lengths, as are my responses to them. Luther encourages flexibility, so I've made no attempt to standardise what happens in the 'thinking out loud' sections that follow. Some 'thinking out loud' sections are longer than others. This is usually for one of two reasons: I found more to say on a passage, or I had more time to devote to the exercise. Again, that's the way it works!

Also remember that this isn't about researching, or about reading commentaries or concordances. Here in these exercises, after prayer, we simply read the word of God and think and reflect out loud before responding in the way that Luther suggests. Because this is a book, my thinking out loud comes (hopefully) as ordered thoughts, but in reality that's not absolutely necessary, and certainly not generally the way it happens. Just think and jot down thoughts as they come, as the Lord reveals them to you.

I'll give you something to consider at the beginning of each exercise, something that might be useful in reading my response and something too that might help you later in your own responses through Chapters 5 and 6. This will include advice on how we might look at a passage: discerning its shape, the main point, and so on. About half way through, I'll leave the final prayer to you as a first step in making this your own. Later, you can have a go at the final two strands of Luther's garland, too.

Two final thoughts, before we begin. First, I would suggest that you don't read this book from now straight through. The exercises are supposed to be discrete portions, so why not read each one reflectively and prayerfully instead?

Second, I should underline here that what follows has a rather objective feel to it because of the public nature of the written and published word. If I were doing this exercise in private I would consider more immediate and personal concerns about myself, my family, my friends, the church I attend, the specific circumstances of the world and so on. It would be both inappropriate and too time-specific here, but remember that the Lord wants us to be 'real' and true to our own circumstances.

Ready to start?

Exodus 19:3–8

Then Moses went up to God, and the Lord called to him from the mountain and said, 'This is what you are to say to the descendants of Jacob and what you are to tell the people of Israel: "You yourselves have seen what I did to Egypt, and how I carried you on eagles' wings and brought you to myself. Now if you obey me fully and keep my covenant, then out of all nations you will be my treasured possession. Although the whole earth is mine, you will be for me a kingdom of priests and a holy nation." These are the words you are to speak to the Israelites.'

So Moses went back and summoned the elders of the people and set before them all the words the Lord had commanded him to speak. The people all responded together, 'We will do everything the Lord has said.'

Thinking out loud

Sometimes we can clearly differentiate characters in a narrative, a discernment that might help us to see what's happening and how helpfully to read the passage. I try this here.

My first thought in reading and rereading this short passage from Exodus is that there are clearly three characters involved in the narrative: God himself; Moses, his servant; and the people of Israel, his people. Following Luther's advice that we always start with God (or with Jesus Christ), I want to begin with him. This makes sense anyway, as he dominates the passage; everything revolves around him and his spoken words—in fact, Moses and the people appear to be defined by his presence and their relationship with him. The fact that Moses 'went *up* to God' is itself indicative of the Lord's position both physically (literally, up at the summit of Mount Sinai) and morally (he is holy, authoritative, to be obeyed) and the movement upwards seems to be a good image of this. He is also described as the God of the whole earth which, again, removes him from our limited thinking and unimaginative theology; our deficient understanding. As Creator of the whole earth and more besides, God possesses the whole earth and everything and everyone in it. He is magnificent! Breathtaking and awesome! To move towards God is to move 'upwards' in so many ways.

This astounding God speaks to Moses. This, itself, is one of the many tremendous and gracious blessings that we experience: God speaks, he reveals himself to us. He accommodates himself to who we are. He talks! His authority is accentuated by the fact that when he speaks he commands allegiance from his people, Israel. He asks them to obey him as he deserves (v. 5). But, interestingly, he does this on the basis, not of his magnificence and grandeur, but of his intimate relationship with the people of Israel. Whereas he judged and destroyed the Egyptians, he carried Israel 'on eagles' wings' (v. 4) and saved them, bringing them to himself. So, significantly, the Lord demands obedience based on his initiating love, his covenant and the historical circumstances of their liberation by the hand of God. He speaks of them as (potentially) his 'treasured possession'— distinguishing them from 'all the nations' (v. 5). It's interesting, and something we don't often remark on, that the Lord speaks of them as his treasured possession *if* they obey him. This is conditional at this point in history, as is their becoming 'a kingdom of priests and a holy nation'. God is busy forming a people for himself at this juncture.

Moses, the second character, is the faithful servant of God. In this passage we see that in the way he climbs the mountain towards God's localised presence and in the way that he responds to God's words that he is to speak to the people. He summons them and 'sets before them all the words the Lord had commanded him to speak' (v. 7). The short phrase '*all* the words' indicates and emphasises his obedience and willingness to serve God. He sets before the people everything the Lord spoke; not a word was forgotten or left out.

The people of Israel are the third 'character' in the passage. The first thing I notice about them is that they have history with the Lord who speaks to them through Moses. Before he calls them 'the people of Israel' (v. 3) he identifies them as 'the descendants of Jacob', which reminds them (and me) that historically they are as progeny included in the covenant that the Lord graciously made with Jacob—they have history! This should give them confidence in the God who calls them 'the descendants of Jacob'; he has already taken the initiative with them in the person of Jacob, he already loves them, has already chosen them. Again, they have history with God in a more recent, immediate manner as he reminds them of his kindness and mercy in liberating them from Egypt 'on eagles' wings' (v. 4). The image of the eagle reminds me of the red kites that fly above my house: free, high, safe, strong, swift and out of reach. The images of being carried on eagles' wings and of being a treasured possession speak of being valued, of being intimately loved, of being cherished and kept safe.

It's fascinating to me that when Moses speaks the words of the Lord to the people they are said to 'respond together', as one people (v. 8). At this point they are obviously enthusiastic and determined to obey the God who has shown them such wonderful mercy. When God asks, 'Will you?' they respond, 'We will!' Grateful hearts respond to grace. I know, of course, that their obedience is short-lived; but the immediacy of their reply demonstrates, at least at this point in their story, their thankfulness and their determination to please the Lord who loves them.

1 Instruction or teaching: What is the Lord seeking to teach me from this passage? What do I need to know?

The main lesson that the Lord teaches me from this short, well-known passage is that he is a God who involves himself in our lives. Here, though he descends to the height of a mountain, he has loved the people of Israel so intimately that he's rescued them from their enemy and now seeks to galvanise that relationship by speaking his will into their lives. The same is true of me. I too have history with the Lord. He has initiated a relationship with me through Jesus Christ; he has rescued me from my enemies (sin, the flesh and the devil, as Luther would say); he has recreated me into a new life by the Holy Spirit. Perhaps there is a shape to our experience of salvation, and it starts with the divine initiative to form a people for himself.

Second, the passage underlines the truth that God speaks. This is something we all too often take for granted, but we shouldn't! That the God who created everything and sustains all things speaks to humanity is an amazing thing. He reveals himself to us. He demonstrates his love by words—and ultimately, of course, by *the* Word, Jesus Christ (see John 1:1–18). The passage shows that he sometimes speaks through intermediaries, like Moses, his servant. That's certainly true today as we hear sermons, prophecies and the like. But he also speaks words to us directly, if we have the ears to hear what the Spirit says to us.

2 Thanksgiving or praise: What should I be grateful for on reading this portion of scripture?

Taking up the two points under 'instruction' above, I'm grateful that the Lord is involved in my life and that he speaks to me. First, I praise the Lord that he is the kind of God (and there is no other!) who is intimately immersed in my daily existence. I praise him as my redeemer; but, more than that, I praise him for not leaving me to my own ways. He is somehow 'entangled' in the detail. Taking the initiative, he cares for me, as he did the people of Israel; he sees me as a treasured possession and I'm immensely thankful.

I'm also thankful that God deigns to speak to us. As I see him speaking to and through Moses I'm grateful that he still speaks today. It reminds me of the importance of the scriptures, through which he speaks his love and care; the importance, too, of faithful sermons gifted with the Spirit's blessing; of words—sometimes apparently casual ones—that speak his grace into situations; of his encouraging voice, heard from time to time in situations of difficulty and distress. Communication indicates relationship; revelation demonstrates love.

3 **Confession or repentance**: How does this passage impinge on my conscience and what in it encourages me to confess particular sins? What sins shall I confess?

I confess that I don't always give God his due. Honestly, I wonder if I ever do, in fact. As for the people of Israel, God has done so much for my salvation. He has loved me with an everlasting love. Through his Spirit he has given me life in all its fullness. Through Jesus Christ he has conquered the grave and given me hope. By speaking to the people of Israel, as he does here, God reminds them of who he is and of who he has been for them. He demands their allegiance on the basis of his outstanding love. The point is, their God is my God; their Saviour is mine. The Lord who speaks to them is the one who reveals himself to me.

Also, I know that too often I find initial enthusiasm for the Lord's words easy. It seems to come naturally. I'll read a passage or hear a powerful sermon and say, as the people of Israel said, 'Yes! I'll obey! I'll follow! I'll be a witness for you, Lord! I'll seek justice! I'll care for the sick!' I have no doubt that the people responded with sincerity, as I do; they wanted to follow God's ways and to obey his word, just like me. Generally, I'm not questioning my sincerity—though at times it's a rather superficial and momentary enthusiasm—but I know only too well how short-lived and fragile that resolve sometimes is. And I confess it in the face of this passage.

4 **Prayer or supplication**: What do I now need to pray for, to cry out to God for?

I need to pray for spiritual insight to know God as he reveals himself and to acknowledge, with thankfulness, his saving love. I need to ask that he shows me anew his involvement in my life and to ask him to commission me again into his mission of life and of justice. I need to cry out for the Holy Spirit to encourage me to a lasting obedience that will glorify his name.

Thinking out loud encourages us to look closely at the passage in front of us and, though we can't really say we have a full understanding of what's happening in this short passage from Exodus 19, we can say that we have a better understanding, an understanding that opens up to the four strands of Luther's simple praying: instruction, thanksgiving/praise, confession and supplication. The strands have personalised what we've discovered because we apply them by asking the pointed and revealing questions. Now comes the prayer, shaped by this exercise, fashioned by it, so that we gain a better grasp of the biblical text and are able to pray accordingly in its light. The prayer doesn't need to use everything we've discovered; though if you have time, it can do.

Loving and covenant-making God, the God who saves, thank you for this passage of scripture. Thank you for revealing yourself to me through your word, revealing yourself as the God intimately involved in my life—historically and today. That's truly amazing! Speak to me your purposes that I might obey you from a heart responding to your grace. Empower me by your wonderful Spirit to live a life that consistently glorifies you. Lead me from my initial enthusiasm and cause me to persist in my obedience. Help me to be your treasured possession, part of your holy nation. Sustain me in my call, that the world will see something of you and of your Son through me. Forgive me for not giving you your due, not acknowledging your eminence, not persevering in the faith more clearly. Accept my heartfelt thanks and praise, O God. Amen

2 Chronicles 30:23–27

The whole assembly then agreed to celebrate the festival seven more days; so for another seven days they celebrated joyfully. Hezekiah king of Judah provided a thousand bulls and seven thousand sheep and goats for the assembly, and the officials provided them with a thousand bulls and ten thousand sheep and goats. A great number of priests consecrated themselves. The entire assembly of Judah rejoiced, along with the priests and Levites and all who had assembled from Israel, including the foreigners who had come from Israel and also those who resided in Judah. There was great joy in Jerusalem, for since the days of Solomon son of David king of Israel there had been nothing like this in Jerusalem. The priests and the Levites stood to bless the people, and God heard them, for their prayer reached heaven, his holy dwelling-place.

Thinking out loud

It's sometimes really helpful to think of a title that would suit a biblical passage. Though this is obviously easier for some passages than for others, it can concentrate our thinking around a particular theme, idea or person. For this extract, it's relatively straightforward.

If I were going to give a title to this short passage, I'd call it 'Joy in worshipping the Lord'. Look at how many times 'joy' is repeated here. Verse 23 tells us that the people are celebrating 'joyfully'. Later, we are told that the entire assembly (plus others) 'rejoiced' (v. 25) and, again, that 'there was great joy in Jerusalem' (v. 26). So joyful was their gathered worship, we are told that 'there had been nothing like this in Jerusalem' (v. 26). It was exceptional worship; nothing like it had been seen in the city in living memory! So I wonder at this point what made the people so joyful; so joyful that it becomes the centrepiece of the passage. What caused them to rejoice in this way and with this seeming exuberance? That's worth considering. I'll come to it again below.

Another thing that strikes me about this passage is that it relates a worship that is costly. The celebrations had been going on for some time before this narrative: it states that the people agreed to celebrate the festival 'seven more days' (v. 23). As we see, this decision came at a price, but obviously they felt that extending their time of worship was worth the cost. What was the cost? Well, for starters, the king, we are told, provided 1,000 more bulls and 7,000 more sheep and goats; the officials provided 1,000 more bulls and 10,000 more sheep and goats. Clearly, they had already provided these animals to sacrifice, but now they provide even more of them. I notice that these are not small numbers! Together with this, the priests seem to have reconsecrated themselves for further festival duty. This worship cost those who celebrated, but the cost didn't dampen their joy.

Again, I wonder what caused their joy during this festival? Could it have been the fact that 'the whole assembly' (v. 23; also v. 25) was gathered; that everyone in Jerusalem was there, seemingly celebrating with one voice, with one accord? I know from being in large worshipping groups of thousands, like at Spring Harvest or Focus, that there is nothing quite like lifting many voices as one to praise the Lord in unison of heart and of faith. There is a 'buzz' of excitement that sometimes literally takes my breath away, leaving me to stand listening to, rather than singing, the songs of praise. The volume itself seems to underline the truth of the singing.

Or, could the joy have come from the fact that there were 'foreigners' among them in their festival of praise to God? The writer is insistent that not only the 'entire assembly of Judah rejoiced' (v. 25) but also included with them were foreigners to the lands of Israel and Judah. The people of Israel and Judah had been commissioned by the Lord to be an example to other nations of what it was like to serve the true and only living God, to draw others to recognise the Lord and to respond in worship of God. Their mission was clear: to be a light in the dark world of their time; to shine forth the truth of the Lord who had saved them for that purpose; to be part of the mission of God himself. To see 'foreigners' among 'the people of God' would bring rejoicing—their mission seeing some success, realising in concrete terms their identity in the Lord's purposes. Joy indeed!

I wonder, though, whether there is something else implied in the passage that speaks of the origin of their joy. As I contemplate what's said here, I think that there is. This is surely hinted at in verse 27, for example, which says that 'the priests and the Levites stood to bless the people, and God heard them, for their prayer reached heaven, his holy dwelling place.' So, though we didn't start with God in the way that Luther might suggest, we've certainly finished with him in a very significant way! God, their God, though he inhabits 'his holy dwelling-place', hears them and blesses them through the priests and Levites. Emphatically, 'their prayer reached heaven'. True worship of this kind is never pointless, never abstract, never devoid of assurance and therefore of joy. I'm reminded of Luther's comments about the Amen that concludes prayer (see Chapter 2). The Amen, he says, is our assurance that prayer has been answered, it gives us confidence that God listens, that he says 'Yes' to what we say. Worship is grounded in an intimate relationship with God; it reaches heaven; it rebounds with gracious divine blessing. It causes rejoicing. True worship brings us joy.

From our thinking out loud on the passage, we might now move to the four strands of Martin Luther's prayer garland: instruction, thanksgiving/praise, confession and supplication.

1 Instruction or teaching: What is the Lord seeking to teach me from this passage? What do I need to know?

The first thing that strikes me from this passage is that worship may cost me! I don't mean that I might be required to supply the sheep or the bulls to offer, of course. But I am aware that too often I enter worship and leave it without having really offered anything. There are Christian believers around the world for whom worship is a costly thing—it may cost them imprisonment, close relationships or even, in extreme situations, their own lives. Worship is costly. And the sacrifices offered in this passage remind me that, for me to worship the Lord 'in the Spirit and in truth' (John 4:23), it actually cost Jesus *his* life! It is through his death and resurrection that I am able to approach God in this way.

This short passage also reminds me that joy comes from knowing that God hears and answers; that *God* hears and answers. The word 'reached' (v. 27) implies a lot. Their prayer 'reached' heaven. It implies that heaven is a long way off and that their prayers just managed to get there; they reached heaven. I used the word in that way when I got to the top of Mount Snowdon in the summer: I reached the summit. It was a struggle, but I managed it. Here, though, it's not seen in terms of distance or difficulty so much as of location or spiritual magnitude or status, perhaps. Their worship reached heaven; it reached God's 'holy dwelling-place' (v. 27). They worshipped and God heard, even from heaven where he dwells in righteousness and glory.

2 Thanksgiving or praise: What should I be grateful for on reading this portion of scripture?

I exalt the Lord for making me a worshipping being, created to enjoy my relationship with him. I praise God for hearing my worship, for hearing my singing and my prayers, and for blessing me through it; for giving me a soul that rejoices in him and that finds real joy in worshipping with his congregation. I recall that the psalmist says, 'My heart and my body cry out for joy to the living God' (Psalm 84:2; NJB)—his whole being is taken up in joyful exaltation, the act of worshipping the Lord, and so is mine!

3 **Confession or repentance**: How does this passage impinge on my conscience and what in it encourages me to confess particular sins? What sins shall I confess?

For all the occasions in which I enjoy worship, and there are many, there are those in which I bring nothing and leave with nothing. I confess that I sometimes come unprepared, with little thought, little preparation, little cost. And, looking at this passage, I realise that often I don't want worship to cost me anything. Too often I want to saunter up to it without due regard for the Lord who calls us to worship. It's all too convenient and without effort. And sometimes I confess that I don't even want to rejoice in God. That's awful to admit! But there it is—sadly, it's sometimes true. (Even in confession, though, I bless the Lord that it's not *always* true of me.)

4 **Prayer or supplication**: What do I now need to pray for, to cry out to God for?

I need to have the Holy Spirit work in grace in my heart in order that I would long to worship the Lord who deserves my wholehearted praise. I pray, too, that the world may come to know God through Jesus Christ and be enabled to worship him and to experience that profound joy.

We now move from thinking out loud to prayer. The prayer doesn't need to use everything we've discovered; though if you have time, it can do.

Amazing and loving God, my Father through Jesus Christ: thank you for hearing my worship, even from heaven. Indeed, elsewhere your scriptures assure me that you inhabit the praises of your people, wonderfully enthroned by them![16] As I worship I come through Jesus Christ—through his costly death and through his resurrection and ascension. I ask that you would inspire me to bring my best to praise you, not half-heartedly, but wholeheartedly, sacrificially, joyfully, spiritually. May the whole of my being—a being that has been created to enjoy you forever—be taken up in praise and adoration of my God. Forgive me my sins in this area and work a work of grace in my heart and life. Through your mercy bring the whole world, all peoples, to give you praise and honour as you deserve and to find enjoyment in their God. Accept my heartfelt thanks and praise, O God. Amen

Psalm 51:1–4

Have mercy on me, O God,
  according to your unfailing love;
according to your great compassion
  blot out my transgressions.
Wash away all my iniquity
  and cleanse me from my sin.
For I know my transgressions,
  and my sin is always before me.
Against you, you only, have I sinned
  and done what is evil in your sight;
So you are right in your verdict
  and justified when you judge.

Thinking out loud

When faced with a rather negative passage like this one, with its repetition of the psalmist's sinfulness, it is sometimes helpful to look carefully for positive signs. Without sidestepping important truths, try not to get trapped into the negative. Scripture is ultimately about divine grace, not judgement. The gospel is 'Yes' not 'No' in Christ. See it everywhere!

This is a well-known start to a penitential psalm that is equally well-known. These few verses instantly raise questions for me, though. One of these is: Why am I so reluctant to confess wrongdoing? Is it because confession is somehow related to punishment in my thinking and past experience; or to shame, to being 'caught out', perhaps? Is it because I picture God as Judge before I see him as Father? In reality, however—and this psalm is a good example of it—I know that true confession to the God who is merciful makes me free; it releases me; it's good for my soul.

I am aware that the goodness of the Lord has been shown in my life, in large part at least in the unqualified forgiveness of my sin. This is why the psalm begins as it does, that God's goodness is demonstrated in the forgiveness of sin. I confess that I used to look at these verses; indeed, I used to preach on them on the subject of sin, and of course that is clearly there (see v. 4). But I realise more and more that I was wrong to single it out as if that were exactly what David was telling us in this private, but very public confession. It's actually much more positive than that. Right at the start of the psalm, he intimates that he is able to approach God simply on the grounds of his—that is, God's—nature. Even as he confesses sinning in the sight of God (v. 4), David acknowledges the divine mercy, his unfailing love, his great compassion (v. 1). Actually, it is very difficult to approach God without being certain of his love and grace. In his day, Luther would say that it was easy to believe there is a God, but more important to believe that that God is *for* us in Christ. So, here, David approaches God only on the basis of divine compassion and mercy. God is for us, not against us! Yes, even in my worst moments, even when it's sometimes difficult to believe.

Confession is such a private thing, and at one level this psalm is intensely personal. But I notice that this psalm becomes very public in the community of faith. In it, David admits to knowing his own sin, using three images to convey his sense of having wronged God (vv. 1–2): 'transgressions' refers to a wilful, self-assertive defiance of God, the equivalent of rebellion; 'iniquity' suggests bending or twisting something that was straight, a distortion of something, a deviation from the right track, putting something out of shape; 'sin' indicates missing the mark through choice, failure.

A good look at these images and reflection on them indicates to me that David is not so much speaking about breaking the law but about distorting his relationship with God. He says, 'Against you, you only, have I sinned' (v. 4). The thing that troubles David so much is not breaking law, as such, but losing the friendship of God, losing his closeness to God. David longs for reality, a clear relationship with his

God. The first line says, 'Have mercy on me, O God!' The word 'mercy' is a word of pleading, from David to God himself; from a sinner to one who is inherently holy and righteous. Interestingly, in this, David acknowledges that the problem is his and his alone, but the only way of transforming the situation is through God alone. It means that he comes to God entirely empty-handed; he has nothing to bargain with, he offers nothing.

Importantly, David recognises that it is God's initiative and ability alone that can bring him back to relationship with him (vv. 1–2). I notice that he uses imperative verbs and images to suggest this: 'have mercy', 'blot out' (erasing words from a scroll or a tablet, maybe even the thought of a debt from a ledger), 'wash away' (pummelling in a river, beating on a rock to eradicate every bit of dirt), 'cleanse' (taking unwanted dross from metal in the furnace to make it pure). But it is *God's* doing, *God's* activity that David calls for, not his own. This is grace in action: *God* having mercy, blotting, washing and cleaning. The psalmist is sure that only the gracious activity of God can bring forgiveness and new life.

I know only too well from experience that sin leaves me an empty shell; it renders me a crippled and powerless Christian. But grace gives me a new life marked by joy, gladness, singing and praise, and divine power to live a life that is extraordinary before him.

From our thinking out loud on the passage, we might now move to the four strands of Martin Luther's prayer garland: instruction, thanksgiving/praise, confession and supplication.

1 Instruction or teaching: What is the Lord seeking to teach me from this passage? What do I need to know?

First, it's necessary for me to be reminded of my own sins and my own rebellion against the Lord who saves. It's against him that I sin. It's *that* relationship that I break. It's a serious matter—one that I shouldn't belittle in any way. Like David and many after him, I must confess when and where my life falls short of open and loving relationship with the Lord.

Second, I need to know the truth that my sin doesn't have the last word on my life. David approaches the Lord for forgiveness. He appears heartbroken because of his sin. But he is certain that seeking the Lord is a positive move of salvation, of deliverance, and he pleads with him for mercy. This is an obvious truth. But I need it drummed into my head and into my life time and time again. I am so slow to learn. Forgiveness comes from God; forgiveness comes from God; forgiveness comes from God! How slow to grasp this cardinal truth of grace! And with forgiveness comes freedom and with freedom joy before the Lord.

2 Thanksgiving or praise: What should I be grateful for on reading this portion of scripture?

I am grateful that we can turn to God and freely find forgiveness: total and ungrudging forgiveness. Though he knows me intimately, as he did David, the Lord is ready to forgive. He's shown that profoundly in Jesus Christ.

3 Confession or repentance: How does this passage impinge on my conscience and what in it encourages me to confess particular sins? What sins shall I confess?

Remember, this isn't the place or the time to list sins; the exercise isn't about that. Here we concentrate on failings that the passage highlights.

I confess that I find it so difficult to move from an intellectual assent of God's goodness—after all, God is love, isn't he?—to a broken, sacrificial, penetrating acknowledgement that he forgives me when I repent and seek his gracious face.[17]

4 Prayer or supplication: What do I now need to pray for, to cry out to God for?

Forgiveness, mercy. I need clarity and perception, too, to see my life as he does. I need humility and openness.

We now move from thinking out loud to prayer. The prayer doesn't need to use everything we've discovered; though if you have time, it can do.

Lord, our gracious God and Father. I trust you who alone can show mercy; who alone can show unfailing love and tremendous, all-sufficient compassion. I acknowledge sin to be troubling me, to be disrupting my life with you, to be sapping spiritual energy and joy from my days. Help me to forfeit myself. Make me humble as your Son Jesus Christ was humble. Empower me with your Holy Spirit and aid me to remove anything that I might consider to be my own righteousness. It is as filthy rags in your sight. I turn to you, the God of grace. Look also to your world in mercy, Lord, and save. Accept my heartfelt thanks and praise, O God. Amen

Isaiah 6:1–8

In the year that King Uzziah died, I saw the Lord, high and exalted, seated on a throne; and the train of his robe filled the temple. Above him were seraphim, each with six wings: with two wings they covered their faces, with two they covered their feet, and with two they were flying. And they were calling to one another:

'Holy, holy, holy is the Lord Almighty;

The whole earth is full of his glory.'

At the sound of their voices the doorposts and thresholds shook and the temple was filled with smoke.

'Woe is me!' I cried. 'I am ruined! For I am a man of unclean lips, and I live among a people of unclean lips, and my eyes have seen the King, the Lord Almighty.'

Then one of the seraphim flew to me with a live coal in his hand, which he had taken with tongs from the altar. With it he touched my mouth and said, 'See, this has touched your lips; your guilt is taken away and your sin is atoned for.'

Then I heard the voice of the Lord saying, 'Whom shall I send? And who will go for us?'

And I said, 'Here am I! Send me!'

Thinking out loud

After reading a passage like this, it's sometimes helpful to begin by gaining an overall impression of what it's saying. What is its big idea? In this case, it's fairly obviously mainly about God himself!

The first overall impression that we gain from this passage is that God is totally awesome. Fascinatingly, it is the Gospel of John that later tells us that it's Jesus' glory that Isaiah sees in this vision (see John 12:41). He is described as 'high and exalted'; he's called 'the Lord Almighty'; seraphs fly around him singing his praises, worshipping him with 'Holy, holy, holy...'; the train of his robe fills the temple. It's significant that he is described here as a king. He's on a throne; he seems to have royal robes on. It's interesting, too, that the scene starts with Isaiah mentioning another king; though this one is human and dying: Uzziah (v. 1). So, the prophet appears to be making a comparison straight away. Though the reference to the king's death may simply be a time-reference, of course, a diary entry placing the vision in a particular year, it may actually be a more significant entry. I was listening to the radio the other week when the announcer said, 'And now Shostakovich's mighty 10th Symphony, written in the year Stalin died.' There was clearly a significance about the two points: 'the mighty 10th Symphony' and Stalin's death. The powerful use of drums and wind instruments seemed to underline the political situation. We see the same thing in the passage. There is a deliberate comparison between a long-lived human king, whose rather successful reign and life had come to an end, with the eternal King of heaven, whose reign will never finish. That would make the point beautifully!

It's fascinating, too, that the prophet sees that the train of God's royal robe fills the temple. It gives the impression that God is so big that even the large temple in Jerusalem could not hold him. Why would he say that? Later, the seraphs sing about the glory of God filling the whole earth! So, there's another comparison here, perhaps. The back part of God's robe fills the temple—the place in which he is worshipped by the Israelite people; the back part, not even the whole robe. Is this an implied criticism? Is God, through the prophet, questioning his people? Even after everything the Lord had done for them, they have such a small view of God. Do they think he is contained in their temple, their religion, somehow limiting him there? Did they feel they somehow owned him? Had they reduced him to their own size? Were they guilty of thinking of him as enclosed, restricted, even tamed, controlled, domesticated and more manageable in their temple? Did they think he was locked into their system; predictable, conforming to their desires, their aspirations? Did they worship the living God too comfortably, too routinely, as a matter of habit, religiously, but not from the heart?

Is that the point? *Their* 'god' fits inside *their* temple. But the living God does not! The vision reveals another, quite different view of 'the King, the Almighty'—one who fills the entire earth with his glory (his presence), one not limited or restricted, an immense God. Perhaps, in a nutshell, the message is that *your God is much too small!*

So God sits as the eternal king, elevated on a throne raised high above the prophet. He is clothed in splendour, surrounded by impressive, heavenly beings—his attendants. God is pictured as an immense, pre-eminent being, one who massively occupies and dominates the throne room, one who fills the whole earth with his glory. This speaks to me of power, authority, eternity, holiness, his glory, the unutterable majesty that is his simply because he is God.

We notice, too, that as the seraphs worship God 'the doorposts and thresholds shook and the temple was filled with smoke'. This reminds me of the scene on Mount Sinai when God gave the ten commandments and the mountain shook and smoke covered it (Exodus 19:18), and also of the nascent church praying in Acts 4 (see 4:31). As they pray they have a similar experience of God's presence— the house shakes, they know they are in the immediate presence of the God to whom they pray, and it's a fearful thing! In this Isaiah passage, the smoke and the doorposts shaking are tangible signs that they stand in the immediate presence of God.

Isaiah's desperate reaction is to fear for his life. He sees God and he is terrified of the odd, overwhelming otherness of God. It's clear that he feels profoundly endangered, exposed, risked. He is utterly unnerved. Isaiah is afraid, knowing that sinful human beings (that's all of us) who see the Lord, who stand in his powerful presence should die because he is holy ('holy, holy, holy,' sing the seraphs earlier—see Psalm 89:5-7, Psalm 103:21): '"Woe is me!" I cried. "I am ruined! For I am a man of unclean lips, and I live among a people of unclean lips, and my eyes have seen the King, the Lord Almighty"' (v. 5).

That's the first impression, but, of course, it's not the only one. Isaiah presents this amazing God as gracious, too. In the prophet's abject fear, God sends a seraph to remind him that standing in the presence of God is a privilege that is God's to give. Symbolically, using coal from the altar, the Lord reminds him that daily his sin is atoned for, his guilt is taken away. What grace! Then he commissions a willing servant into mission; he sends a prophet to do the Lord's work among his people.

There is more in this wonderful and well-known passage, but we easily have enough to move to the four strands of Martin Luther's prayer garland: instruction, thanksgiving/praise, confession and supplication.

1 Instruction or teaching: What is the Lord seeking to teach me from this passage? What do I need to know?

First, the main lesson for me is that God is totally awesome; he is an amazing God. The holy God is not to be surveyed casually as an object. He is not to be worshipped without a sense of who it is to whom we give our praise and adoration. To this God every knee will bow and every tongue will confess him to be Lord (see Philippians 2:9–11).

Second, this is about ourselves (notice the order: God first, then ourselves). Isaiah is suddenly and brutally aware of himself. He is personally confronted with the Holy God. I remember climbing a mountain in Scotland and at the top being overawed by the truly spectacular view, realising my own smallness and insignificance in comparison. Not that I am insignificant—none of us are (see Psalm 8:5)—but that *in comparison* with the height and massive size of the mountain, the expansive view, I felt it. So, here, Isaiah sees himself before and in the sight of the living God. The finite, mortal, incomplete, fallible, sinful human being encounters the infinite, eternal, self-consistent, infallible and holy God. That is to know something of one's own self and existence. The Lord wants us to see ourselves as we really are before him.

Third, grace comes from God. The passage underlines that all the spiritual benefits we enjoy daily come directly from God; they don't proceed in any way from me. So forgiveness, atonement, deliverance, redemption, spiritual life, the divine call into mission of whatever sort, and other signs of God's goodness stem from the Lord's grace or kindness and mercy. As we saw above, this is a prominent theme in Luther's theology. In line with the New Testament, he links this with Jesus Christ in whom, he says, we have everything.

2 Thanksgiving or praise: What should I be grateful for on reading this portion of scripture?

If I think carefully about this, I want to express my utter astonishment at who God is and who he reveals himself to be here—actually, the very fact that he does reveal himself to me in this way. He's an amazing God, filling the entire earth with his presence, massive in his being, gracious but perplexing, infinite and kind. I realise that this is 'the tip of the iceberg', as it were. This doesn't come close to describing God as he is—it's an image—but gives an impression that I can understand and grasp. He is much, much 'more' than this.

I'm grateful that everything good comes from this amazing God. As I read of the seraph approaching the prophet Isaiah and the voice saying that his sins are atoned for, I'm grateful that this reminds me that my sins, too, are atoned for, that my guilt has been done away with, just as the prophet's was. I know myself; I know how far short of what God wants for me I come, yet I'm assured of his love and grace. He knows me, as he knew Isaiah, yet he gives me everything in Christ, freely, without cost.

3 **Confession or repentance**: How does this passage impinge on my conscience and what in it encourages me to confess particular sins? What sins shall I confess?

I know I really don't have this view of God in my mind all the time. My God becomes too small, particularly when it's convenient to have a domesticated 'god', a god I can determine, a god I can put in my pocket and silence when I want things my way, and not his. But God is immense, powerful, with authority. I confess that I minimise him to my own advantage at times. (I might think of specific examples here.)

Sometimes, and too often, I think I can do this spiritual thing all by myself. I can't! When I sin I think I have to make up to God and that will somehow put things right: I read scripture, I pray, I try to do good things—perhaps that will sort matters out with God. But this passage reminds me rather forcefully that it is God alone who puts things right, who sorts things out. He alone sustains me in his love and grace.

4 **Prayer or supplication**: What do I now need to pray for, to cry out to God for?

I need his help to know him as he is. I can't do this myself; I rely on his revelation to show me just what he is like as God. I need grace every day. Again, this comes from the gracious God alone. I need forgiveness, a new start and calling into his mission in whatever form that may take.

We now move from thinking out loud to prayer. The prayer doesn't need to use everything we've discovered; though if you have time, it can do.

Our God, what an amazing God you are! Your glory, your presence fills the earth. I am astonished that you reveal yourself to us in ways we can understand. Thank you for reminding me that you are far, far bigger than I normally anticipate. I have such a diminished view of you at times. I'm truly sorry for that. It's dishonouring to you, O God. And I realise that everything I have comes from your gracious hand—I'm forgiven, saved, redeemed and made free, not because of things I've done or could accomplish, but simply because you've shown your love towards me. Forgive me, please, for believing that I add anything to my own salvation. Again, that's so dishonouring to you, O God of atoning grace. Help me to demonstrate the love of such a God to the world in which I live. Accept my heartfelt thanks and praise, O God. Amen

Lamentations 3:19–26, 31–32

I remember my affliction and my wandering,
  the bitterness and the gall.
I well remember them,
  and my soul is downcast within me.
Yet this I call to mind
  and therefore I have hope.
Because of the Lord's great love we are not consumed,
  for his compassions never fail.
They are new every morning;
  great is your faithfulness.
I say to myself, 'The Lord is my portion;
  therefore I will wait for him.'
The Lord is good to those whose hope is in him,
  to the one who seeks him;
it is good to wait quietly
  for the salvation of the Lord...
For no one is cast off
  by the Lord forever.
Though he brings grief, he will show compassion,
  so great is his unfailing love.

Thinking out loud

Sometimes passages present us with tension. It is palpable in this one. Recognise tension and try to keep it in balance as you look at the passage.

There is clear tension here. The writer (Jeremiah, the prophet), in grave difficulties, reminds himself that God is loving towards him *despite* his awful present circumstances. In this short passage he speaks of 'the Lord's great love', his goodness, his compassion and his faithfulness. The New Testament speaks of God as love

(1 John 4:8); love is a characteristic of his essential being, that's who he is. His love is seen as goodness here as he extends his care to the prophet. It's termed 'grace' too—God's love towards us as sinners, undeserved love. In Luther's well-worn statement, grace means God is *for* us, *not* against us. Faith looks beyond present circumstances and believes that God is for us (see Psalm 56:9). Because he loves us, because he deals with us in grace, not judgement, we know that God is faithful: he is the same yesterday, today and forever,[18] consistently on our side, his promises are always fulfilled—he does what he says he'll do—he is absolutely reliable. He is entirely trustworthy.

And yet, the writer's 'soul is downcast' within him. He seems to be brooding on that, even agonising over it. The statement that it is his 'soul' that is so low seems to add weight to this—it seems as if the whole of his being is affected by sorrow, bitterness and grief. There is a depth of experience here.[19] This isn't just a minor irritation or a superficial grumble; his entire being seems to be taken up with the dreadful situation he finds himself in. In verse 32 he speaks of the Lord as bringing the grief upon him. (I'm leaving that to one side for now, like the barn that Holman Hunt's student was painting; it will still be there tomorrow.) Taking it at face value, perhaps Jeremiah is saying that God is so big, so imponderable, that his own life in its entirety is in the divine purpose. The point for now is that his pain, his distress is intolerable to him. The first two verses (vv. 19–20) spell out grief, vulnerability, rejection and a loss of peace, all of which consume him—graphically, he feels 'cast off' (v. 31). This last phrase is particularly vivid, pointing as it does to feeling thrown aside; it's more than abandoned, which would seem rather passive in comparison.

Here is a a godly person, who grieves and laments, weary, troubled and humiliated, distressed and suffering—crushed and heartbroken—in a situation that I can only just begin to imagine. In a small way, it reminds me of times in my own life when God seemed distant and when everything was fractured and out of joint. This concentrated passage, reflected to an extent in my own experience, witnesses to the fact of humanity's suffering and it reminds me that suffering is a huge and unavoidable element in the fallen human condition. It seems that to be human is to suffer. But, perhaps, to be godly is to remember that even in such dire circumstances God is still faithful—trustworthy, reliable. God is always *for us* as he says he will be.

Amazingly, here, in the midst of the tragic, bitter, crushing situation, Jeremiah speaks verses 21–26 about the love and faithfulness of God. Two phrases stand out for me. The first is in verse 21 where he says, 'Yet this I call to mind'. Here is a conscious decision in the context of distress 'to call to mind'. He decides to bring to the fore; he consciously remembers. It's as if he digs around in his memory for some hope and sees the divine faithfulness. And this is not the prophet simply saying, as I do too often, I can find a verse of scripture that reminds me of God's faithfulness. Rather, it is the writer saying that he's previously experienced the faithfulness of God and so now his hope rests on God himself.

The second phrase that stands out is, 'The Lord is my portion' (v. 24). Again, there is a sense of genuine relationship and confidence in God himself. It's significant that both these phrases end with a 'therefore', with a consequence! 'Yet this I call to mind and *therefore* I have hope' (v. 21). 'The Lord is my portion, *therefore* I will wait for him' (v. 24). Because the Lord's 'steadfast love never ceases', because his 'mercies never come to an end', because they are 'new every morning' the writer has hope and he waits for the Lord's presence and a turnaround of his circumstances. He knows that 'the Lord is good to those whose hope is in him' (v. 25); that those who wait quietly for salvation (deliverance from the specific situation in this case) will see the goodness of God (v. 26).

This is clearly not simply a stoical response. That he's decided to hope and to wait on the Lord doesn't stop the writer from moaning, from lamenting the terrible situation—but he *decides* in the situation to look to God who is faithful all the time. He waits for him, he seeks him, he prays, he worships, he anticipates his deliverance.

(If I had time, I'd like to remind myself here that God's faithfulness is seen most clearly in Jesus Christ. God's promises are 'Yes and Amen' in him (see 2 Corinthians 1:19). Though this is outside our text, it reminds us of Luther's insistence on keeping Jesus central to our biblical reading. God's faithfulness can be measured by his commitment to his promises—to fulfil his promise of salvation he 'did not spare his own Son', says Paul in Romans 8:32.)

From our thinking out loud on the passage, we might now move to the four strands of Martin Luther's prayer garland: instruction, thanksgiving/praise, confession and supplication.

1 Instruction or teaching: What is the Lord seeking to teach me from this passage? What do I need to know?

I am so prone to think of God as faithful because things are going well. I need to learn that God is faithful in good *and* in difficult times. The writer here clearly remembers God's faithfulness in past times (Were they good or difficult? We don't know—realistically, probably a mixture of both) and applies that in his agony to bolster his faith and hope in the Lord. God is faithful when life is good. God is faithful when we are suffering. God is faithful in our salvation, in our life, in our death and in eternity. I need to know that as I've experienced it on numerous occasions in my Christian life.

The passage also reminds me that believers suffer and may complain in prayer as a result. We suffer because we're caught up in a broken creation, but scripture shows godly men and women struggling with that fact and greatly troubled by it. They show their frustration through lament—this portion of Lamentations is a fine example, as are many of the psalms. Godly complaint is entirely appropriate in a fallen world. But the passage teaches us that complaint doesn't negate our awareness of God's love; rather, it is spoken in that context.

2 **Thanksgiving or praise**: What should I be grateful for on reading this portion of scripture?

I exalt the Lord because he's faithful in everything and in every circumstance. Above and beyond trying and difficult experiences there is someone who cares for the fallen and the vexed. I bless him as a faithful Father, even when life is tough.

3 **Confession or repentance**: How does this passage impinge on my conscience and what in it encourages me to confess particular sins? What sins shall I confess?

Looking at how the prophet trusts in the faithfulness of God, seemingly against the evidence of the situation, I question whether I have this faith and assurance. I am too prone to allow circumstances and mood to determine what I think of God. In truth, that's terrible. In all his distress and grief, the writer makes that vital decision to trust in a God he knows to be faithful.

4 **Prayer or supplication**: What do I now need to pray for, to cry out to God for?

I need to pray for a consistent faith that looks beyond circumstances to the God of the Bible; or, better, to the God I know through experience of his saving love.

We now move from thinking out loud to prayer. The prayer doesn't need to use everything we've discovered; though if you have time, it can do.

Gracious and faithful God, I look to you in the midst of today's concerns. At times my own situation seems difficult, fraught with imponderable matters that I simply can't solve. Teach me to rely on you. Teach me to trust you as a faithful Father.

Remind me by your loving Spirit of times in which you've blessed me by your presence. Empower me to decide to trust. Lord, the broken world is a mess right now. Your world. Wars, famine, terrible acts of violence, lies and pride. When, O Lord, will it cease? When will you come in power and deliverance? When will peace, your peace, reign throughout the world? Come, Lord Jesus. Come and bring the peace you promised. Bring salvation to the world. Bring joy and praise. Accept my heartfelt thanks and praise, O God. Amen

Ezekiel 37:1–10

The hand of the Lord was on me, and he brought me out by the Spirit of the Lord and set me in the middle of a valley; it was full of bones. He led me to and fro among them, and I saw a great many bones on the floor of the valley, bones that were very dry. He asked me, 'Son of man, can these bones live?'

I said, 'Sovereign Lord, you alone know.'

Then he said to me, 'Prophesy to these bones and say to them, "Dry bones, hear the word of the Lord! This is what the Sovereign Lord says to these bones: I will make breath enter you, and you will come to life. I will attach tendons to you and make flesh come upon you... and you will come to life. Then you will know that I am the Lord."'

So I prophesied as I was commanded. And as I was prophesying, there was a noise, a rattling sound, and the bones came together, bone to bone. I looked, and tendons and flesh appeared on them and skin covered them, but there was no breath in them.

Then he said to me... 'Prophesy, son of man, and say to it, "This is what the sovereign Lord says: come, breath, from the four winds and breathe into these slain, that they may live."' So I prophesied as he commanded me, and breath entered them; they came to life and stood up on their feet—a vast army.

Then he said to me: 'Son of man, these bones are the people of Israel. They say, "Our bones are dried up and our hope is gone; we are cut off." Therefore prophesy and say to them: "This is what the Sovereign Lord says: my people, I am going to open your graves and bring you up from them; I will bring you back to the land of Israel. Then you, my people, will know that I am the Lord, when I open your graves and bring you up from them. I will put my Spirit in you and you will live,

and I will settle you in your own land. Then you will know that I the Lord have spoken, and I have done it, declares the Lord."'

Thinking out loud

Familiar passages (and songs) present their own difficulty. Be careful to take from the passage what's there, not what we seem to remember is there!

What a wonderful passage this is. This is a vision of hope, life and renewed purpose; but we notice that it evolves from a circumstance of hopelessness and despair. The people of Israel, represented in the vision by the dry bones, lament their situation: 'Then he said to me: "Son of man, these bones are the people of Israel. They say, 'Our bones are dried up and our hope is gone; we are cut off'"' (v. 11). The situation seems to be the exile, for God promises their return: 'I will settle you in your own land' (v. 14). Gracious God sees their plight and hears their lament (v. 11) and gives the prophet, Ezekiel, a vision in response (vv. 1–10).

The vision is of a valley scattered with dry and lifeless bones. The emphasis on their dryness suggests, perhaps, that they have been baked in the hot sun over a long time. Despite its ending, the scene begins predominantly as one of death, decay and uncleanness—a setting that a priest like Ezekiel would want to avoid at all costs. The Old Testament law forbade a priest to touch anything that was dead or decaying, so he would have avoided it as abhorrent to him. Here, though, God actually takes Ezekiel into the place of death, 'setting him in the middle of a valley' (v. 1), in the heart of death itself.

To God's question about dead bones living, the prophet answers (paraphrased), 'You know the answer to that. Of course they can't live!' (v. 3), which suggests, of course, that he hasn't yet learned the lesson about the greatness and power of God, the sovereign Lord. So he's told to 'Prophesy to these bones!' and eventually the dry, dead bones come to life as the spirit of God is breathed into them: they stand on their feet, a vast army (v. 10).

It's tempting to read this as a parable or vision about resurrection, and though it might remind us of that important truth it's not about resurrection; it's about restoration, new life, hope, trust and purpose. It gives extraordinary insight into the life-giving capacity of God. To these people whose life seemed over, pointless, useless, there is declared the possibility of new life, new possibilities and new horizons.

God appears to give the vision for a single reason, but in relation to two people: the prophet and the people of Israel. The reason he gives the vision is to demonstrate that he is the sovereign Lord. To the prophet Ezekiel he says, 'Then [after the bones come to life] you will know that I am the Lord' (v. 6). To the people he says the same thing twice: 'Then [when they are brought back to their land] you, my people, will know that I am the Lord' (v. 13); and, later, 'Then [when the Spirit lives in them and they are sent home] you will know that I the Lord have spoken, and I have done it' (v. 14). This suggests to me that Ezekiel, though he knew God, hadn't the faith that God could do this amazing thing. The Lord wants him to remember the vision when he speaks to a lamenting people. He is God, and he can do what he says or promises; he has that power and that ability. It is essential that the people receive this vision of encouragement so that in their abject despair they retain a realistic hope of God's vivifying grace. He is God! He can restore them to life and hope, to a future in their own land. Indeed, that is his purpose.

Something else I notice from this passage is the place of the Spirit of God in all that happens. In verse 1 we are told that the Spirit of the Lord sets the prophet down in the valley. In Hebrew, the word *ruach* means spirit, Spirit, wind, breath. It's fascinating, then, that we have a rather pervasive ambiguity throughout the chapter about this. Verses 5 and 6 suggest that 'breath' from the Lord brings the bones together. A little later, the prophet is told by the Lord to prophesy to the breath: 'come, breath, from the four winds and breathe into these slain, that they may live' (v. 9). Breath enters them and they come to life (v. 10). And, finally, to his people the Lord says, 'I will put my Spirit in you and you will live' (v. 14). This speaks to me of the centrality and necessity of the work of the Holy Spirit in our lives as believers. He is life. He gives us freedom and purpose. He takes us from our brokenness and unresponsiveness and sets us on our feet.

From our thinking out loud on the passage, we might now move to the four strands of Martin Luther's prayer garland: instruction, thanksgiving/praise, confession and supplication.

1 Instruction or teaching: What is the Lord seeking to teach me from this passage? What do I need to know?

The first thing that I need to know is that God sees and speaks. The passage encourages me to realise again the amazing love of God for his people, for me. He obviously cares, he is concerned about where we are on our journey. Here, he loves even a rebellious, seemingly dead, people! So he cares for me, even when I'm at a distance from him, dead to all intents and purposes, rebellious. I notice, too, that his speaking into this situation is creative. Just as in creation God's command brings light, land, animals, vegetation, humanity into being, so his speech here radically changes the situation. There is, in God's word, the ability and the power to accomplish what he intends, what is spoken.

Fascinating, as well, is the fact that God is not distant, but with his word he enters into the circumstances of his people. In Ezekiel 37 he enters into the plight of his people to bring them hope—he does this through his prophet and through vision and exhortation. It reminds me, of course, that in Jesus Christ, the Word of God, the Lord speaks into the situation of fallen humanity: 'He was *in* the world, and the world came into being through him; yet the world did not know him. He came *to* what was his own...' (John 1:10–11, NRSV, emphasis added), 'And the Word became flesh and *lived among us*' (v. 14, emphasis added), revealing grace and truth.

The second thing that I need to know from this passage is that God is the God of life. Here, marvellously, in Ezekiel, he brings dead and dry bones to life. His promise is to bring passionless Israel to life through his Spirit within them. They are dead, but through his power they stand. The life the Lord brings is life in all its fullness. Too often the world teaches us to be the driving force of our own destiny; culture stresses our independence—'be your own person', 'just do it'—but scripture assures us that life in all its richness is derived only from God, through Jesus Christ (see, particularly, for example, John 1:2–31 and John 1:1–2).

Third, Ezekiel 37 reminds me, particularly, that restored life derives from the Lord's goodness, too. It reminds me that I can't simply 'pull my socks up' when I'm in despair or sensing a lack of enthusiasm in spiritual things. I need to pray that the Lord of life might restore me to a new hope and a new purpose, as he did so magnificently with Israel here. I need to listen to his Spirit. I need to hear and to respond to grace.

2 Thanksgiving or praise: What should I be grateful for on reading this portion of scripture?

I'm grateful because this passage underlines the fact that all life comes from God. Just as physical life originates from him, so does spiritual life.[20] I praise the Lord for his interventions in my life— tangible signs of his love. He has given me life, brought me to new birth in Christ, restored me when I've fallen, given me a life of purpose and of certain hope in him.

3 **Confession or repentance**: How does this passage impinge on my conscience and what in it encourages me to confess particular sins? What sins shall I confess?

I confess that I'm not as conscious as I ought to be about the wonderful gift of life, in all its aspects. I take for granted my physical existence, for example, not thanking God for every new day he bestows upon me. I'm the same with my spiritual life sometimes, neglecting the fact that Jesus died to give it to me in all its fullness.

4 **Prayer or supplication**: What do I now need to pray for, to cry out to God for?

I pray that the Lord would enrich my understanding of what it means to be given life in all its fullness. Restore me again by the breath of your mouth, your Holy Spirit—make these dead bones live. And, as I pray for myself, I beseech the Lord for my family and friends, for his church and for his world. The world is given life from God, but it remains exiled from God its creator, missing the fullness of life—not simply a question of heaven and hell, but of life in its fullness now, today, experiencing Jesus Christ's love by his Spirit.

We now move from thinking out loud to prayer. The prayer doesn't need to use everything we've discovered; though if you have time, it can do. Perhaps you'd like to read the passage again, and what's been said here, and form your own prayer. Use what's been said, but also write your own thoughts down, too; and pray them.

Mark 4:35–41

That day when evening came, [Jesus] said to his disciples, 'Let us go over to the other side.' Leaving the crowd behind, they took him along, just as he was, in the boat. There were also other boats with him. A furious squall came up, and the waves broke over the boat, so that it was nearly swamped. Jesus was in the stern, sleeping on a cushion. The disciples woke him and said to him, 'Teacher, don't you care if we drown?'

He got up, rebuked the wind and said to the waves, 'Quiet! Be still!' Then the wind died down and it was completely calm.

He said to his disciples, 'Why are you so afraid? Do you still have no faith?'

They were terrified and asked each other, 'Who is this? Even the wind and the waves obey him!'

Thinking out loud

Sometimes it's good to start by simply retelling the story in a few words. It can concentrate our thinking on the narrative. That way, we might get the hang of what's happening.

Let's try that here.

At the end of the day, Jesus asks his disciples to go with him to the other side of the lake, leaving the crowd—and the opportunities—behind. The boat they are in becomes embroiled in a vicious storm, causing the disciples to panic in fear. They wake Jesus up (surprisingly, he's been sleeping through it all) and appear to accuse him of not caring. He calms the storm and accuses *them* of having insubstantial faith. They are overawed by the man.

There is no doubt that Mark tells this story to centre our thinking on Jesus himself. He is clearly the dominant figure in the story—the final rhetorical question from his disciples, 'Who is this?' (v. 41), makes this certain and encourages us to ask and to answer it in our turn. But there is a lot going on before we get to that.

This short scene moves rather dramatically from calmness (Jesus leaving the crowd of people behind, v. 36) through difficulties (the storm, the disciples' consequent fear) to calm again ('the wind died down and it was completely calm', v. 39). The difficulties in this case are described briefly but powerfully as a 'furious squall' that 'broke over the boat, so that it was nearly swamped' (v. 37). Mark makes sure we understand the situation: the calm with which the vignette opens and closes seems explicitly to be in contrast to the disciples' troubles. Mark makes sure that we understand that the storm was enough to make them fear for their lives—I note their rather crass, blundering question, addressed to Jesus, 'Don't you care if we drown?' (v. 38).

Their question seems a little personal, doesn't it? Don't you *care*? Aren't you bothered about us? Aren't we worth your worry? As if Jesus was sleeping in the boat without concern for his own disciples' lives! The question appears to cast doubt on Jesus' love and commitment for them. And this is surely stabbing at the very heart of the relationship initiated by Jesus in the first place. Who could question his love? Then I think of times in my own life when I've hit rock bottom and done the identical thing, doubting God's (Jesus') love for me, and I realise again how easy and how human it all is, and how lacking in true faith. Jesus pinpoints this in his rebuke of the disciples after stilling the waves and the wind: 'Why are you so afraid? Do you still have no faith?' (v. 40).

In today's church climate, we seem only too willing to question God in times of trouble; we doubt whether he's really there for us, whether he really cares. In some circles this is actually encouraged. We say it's somehow being real. It's an easy option—I've been guilty of that myself. But Jesus, it seems, will have none of it. He rebukes the disciples for their lack of faith: notice, 'Do you still have *no* faith?' And, of course, it is this reproach, together with the miracle, that causes the disciples to fear Jesus: 'They were terrified,' Mark says (v. 41).

As easily as Jesus brings calm to created things—the strong winds and the tumultuous waves—so he can bring calm to every situation that I face. His rebuke notwithstanding, Jesus' critical words seek to encourage faith in his disciples, as does Mark's inclusion of the event in his short Gospel.

From our thinking out loud on the passage, we might now move to the four strands of Martin Luther's prayer garland: instruction, thanksgiving/praise, confession and supplication.

1 Instruction or teaching: What is the Lord seeking to teach me from this passage? What do I need to know?

I need to know that Jesus is totally trustworthy, as did his disciples. As he sleeps in the boat they begin to doubt this truth, fearing for their lives. Jesus reassures them by word and deed: he rebukes them as one with authority; and that same authority is turned upon the waves and the wind. Not only is he the Lord of creation (after all, everything was created through him), but he demands to be Lord of my life too. He claims my faith in difficult times, my trust in every circumstance.

2 Thanksgiving or praise: What should I be grateful for on reading this portion of scripture?

Simply put, I am thankful for Jesus Christ. I'm grateful that he has inherent authority. I'm grateful too that he protects me because he loves me, just as he did the disciples. I can turn to him in times of difficulty, in stressful circumstances, in fear, in grief and sorrow—in death itself.

3 **Confession or repentance**: How does this passage impinge on my conscience and what in it encourages me to confess particular sins? What sins shall I confess?

I confess to being like the disciples on too many occasions, when I've accused Jesus for not doing enough, for not being there for me, for not really caring. As with them, I need to trust more—to believe he is who he says he is, the Son of God. I'm sorry that I don't believe this enough to allow it to make a distinct difference to my day-to-day living. Why do I fear circumstances more than I fear God?

4 **Prayer or supplication**: What do I now need to pray for, to cry out to God for?

I would pray for God's Holy Spirit to enlarge my vision of Jesus and to make me trust him with the whole of my being. Don't permit situations to loom so large that they take my focus off the love and grace of God in Jesus Christ.

We now move from thinking out loud to prayer. The prayer doesn't need to use everything we've discovered; though if you have time, it can do. Again, as above, perhaps you'd like to reread the passage, and what's been said here, and form your own prayer. Use what's been said, but also write your own thoughts down, too; and pray them.

Luke 15:11–24

Jesus continued: 'There was a man who had two sons. The younger one said to his father, "Father, give me my share of the estate." So he divided his property between them.

'Not long after that, the younger son got together all he had, set off for a distant country and there squandered his wealth in wild living. After he had spent everything, there was a severe famine in that whole country, and he began to be in need. So he went and hired himself out to a citizen of that country, who sent him to his fields to feed pigs. He longed to fill his stomach with the pods that the pigs were eating, but no one gave him anything.

'When he came to his senses, he said, "How many of my father's hired servants have food to spare, and here I am starving to death! I will set out and go back to my father and say to him: Father, I have sinned against heaven and against you. I am no longer worthy to be called your son; make me like one of your hired servants." So he got up and went to his father.

'But while he was still a long way off, his father saw him and was filled with compassion for him; he ran to his son, threw his arms round him and kissed him.

'The son said to him, "Father, I have sinned against heaven and against you. I am no longer worthy to be called your son."

'But the father said to his servants, "Quick! Bring the best robe and put it on him. Put a ring on his finger and sandals on his feet. Bring the fattened calf and kill it. Let's have a feast and celebrate. For this son of mine was dead and is alive again; he was lost and is found." So they began to celebrate.'

Thinking out loud

Sometimes it's a good idea to take each verse at a time and to concentrate on exactly what's happening. This takes time, of course, but can reap clear and detailed focus. So I'm going to look at this well-known parable in this way, reflecting on one or two verses at a time as the narrative unfolds.

This is definitely one of my favourite passages of scripture. It speaks to me so powerfully—the early sharp juxtaposition and the final bringing together of a faithless, abandoning son and the gracious, merciful father. It took many years of being a Christian before I really learned what the fatherhood of God meant to me as a son of divine grace, before I knew it enough to trust in that relationship.[21]

Luke 15:11–12 The opening situation is simply unthinkable to me: it seems to amount to the son saying to his father, 'The only good you are to me is your money. I can't wait for you to die.' In fact, he is treating his father as if he was already dead. This is an extraordinary and shocking insult. I can't imagine making this callous comment, nor hearing it, and I think that's the point. This verbal slap in the face destroys any relationship that might have existed between the two men. I expect the father to explode in anger at the insult, to refuse the request and to punish his son. In a simple phrase, 'So he divided his property between them' (v. 12b), remarkably, the father shows vulnerable love: he allows the son to reject him, he grants him the 'freedom' he desires.[22]

Luke 15:13a Two things stand out to me here. First, the son thinks he is now wealthy, independent, able to run his own life; that he has everything he needs. The irony is that he's actually impoverished himself.[23] Just like the younger son, we are often very slow to grasp this. I recall a home group many years ago and one older member lamenting that he'd wished that he'd waited before giving his life to the Lord and then he could have 'lived a bit', as he put it. Is that how I see my life? Somehow restricted by being a Christian? Yet, in Jesus,

God offers us 'life in all its fullness'. Second, the younger son rejects his own people. He goes into a distant country—evidently, a land of Gentiles. So the insult is not just to the father (that's bad enough), but to the whole village, the entire extended family. He has disregarded really important and significant loyalties; he has broken relationships. He has earned the displeasure of the whole community.

Luke 13b–14 Is this what freedom looks like? A single Jew, vulnerable in a foreign country, unable to look after himself—a powerful image to a people who had been exiled in foreign lands. They knew what it was like. It was part of their communal narrative, their identity, almost of their DNA.

Luke 15:15–16 It is hard for me to feel the revulsion that the Jews had towards pigs. By Jesus' day they had become a symbol of paganism. In this turn of events, Jesus demonstrates the younger son's desperation. The circumstances in which he now finds himself are basically forcing him to renounce his own religion.

Luke 15:17–19 He came to the end of his tether—a stark realisation of the situation. So, ultimately motivated by hunger, he repents of losing his money and independence. 'I am no longer worthy to be called your son. Make me like one of your hired servants.' He returns because he has lost all his money and is starving to death in a Gentile land. The Lord uses circumstances to encourage my return, too.

Luke 15:20 Surely, this is the most amazing verse of the parable. He gets up and goes to his father; the man whom he insulted, the man whom he rejected outright and publicly. 'But while he was still a long way off, his father saw him and was filled with compassion for him; he ran to his son, threw his arms round him and kissed him.' In Jesus' day, great and noble men didn't run; it was unheard of. But here is the father running because he's seen from a distance his son returning. Several things are worth reflecting on here. The father has obviously been looking for his son's return because he has compassion—he has sympathy, kindness and concern for him, even though he'd been hurt by his behaviour. Also, in throwing his arms around the miscreant son and kissing him in public, the father protects the son from the potential hostility of the community which he'd rejected. He is also welcoming him home without qualification and without grudge. The son receives humble and vulnerable love from the one he'd hurt most. Total acceptance.

Luke 15:21–24 The son's well-rehearsed speech is cut short. He realises that the point is a broken relationship, which he cannot heal. All he can utter is, 'I am not worthy'. It's at this point, of course, that Jesus gives us a picture of the outpouring of grace, of love visibly demonstrated. The father calls for the best robe (almost certainly the father's own) to be put around the son; a ring (a sign of trust—'the family ring', *THE MESSAGE*) on his finger; sandals (a sign of being free, not a servant) on his feet; and the cooking of a fattened calf in order to rejoice with the whole community on the son's return. 'For this son of mine was dead and is alive again; he was lost and is found.' The son accepts the undeserved but generous love of his father on his father's terms. 'So they began to celebrate.' Amazing.

From our thinking out loud on the passage, we might now move to the four strands of Martin Luther's prayer garland: instruction, thanksgiving/praise, confession and supplication.

1 Instruction or teaching: What is the Lord seeking to teach me from this passage? What do I need to know?

As I reflect I'll list several things that have struck me as important for me at the moment, given that it's a parable about divine grace.

1 Grace indicates that God is for us, not against us (see Romans 8:31). We've seen this theme previously, but it's absolutely central to the Bible. Martin Luther rejoiced in this truth, as we've seen. Similarly, I can't repeat it too often. So, essentially, the parable's teaching is that grace indicates that God is for us who, in our

fallen selves, are so often against him. That, to me, is one of the amazing things about the grace of God. Grace is free and totally undeserved. By grace God makes enemies, those hostile to him, his friends. As this parable demonstrates, grace involves love, compassion, generosity, forgiveness and much, much more. Grace deals with us where we are and according to our need. It does so only on the basis of the goodness and the overwhelming generosity of God. Grace is shorthand for 'God giving himself'.

2 The grace of God is so rich it appears as 'extravagant'. It is grace that overflows, that exceeds all expectation; a grace that simply astounds its recipients—like the younger son in this story, like me time and time and time again.

3 Grace leaves God vulnerable. Seen pre-eminently in Jesus Christ, God incarnate. Philip Yancey, in his remarkable book, *What's so Amazing about Grace*, says simply and memorably, 'I marvel at a God who allows himself to endure such humiliation.'[24] Grace baffles me!

4 Grace gives us second chances. This is so clear in the parable. The son is given dignity; he is restored to the family, he is once again the father's son. No, he's always been the father's son—now he takes his familial position. The prodigal had everything that the father had, and he returns to the same. Grace takes us and puts us in a place of unearned and undeserved dignity.

2 Thanksgiving or praise: What should I be grateful for on reading this portion of scripture?

I'm grateful for the Lord's love and compassion towards me, especially at times when I've let him down, forsaken his paths, and gone my own way. I know what it is to be a prodigal son. I know what it is to return in sorrow and repentance, humbled before him, sensing the Lord's gracious welcome. I'm thankful that he never gave up on me, but waited, hurting and longing—as the vulnerable father does here in the parable Jesus told. Thank you for second chances; for extravagant grace.

3 Confession or repentance: How does this passage impinge on my conscience and what in it encourages me to confess particular sins? What sins shall I confess?

In confessing, I'm forced to ask questions of myself: Am I overwhelmed by the grace of God as I should be? Do I trust the grace of God? Does my life radiate faith, joy, gratitude, love and praise for the grace freely showered on me in Jesus Christ? Is my life reflective of the transforming nature of the grace of God? What of God's grace do I offer the prodigal? The rhetorical nature of these questions is my confession.

4 Prayer or supplication: What do I now need to pray for, to cry out to God for?

I need to pray about my own attitude to divine grace, of course; but, I need to pray for the church's generosity, reflecting God's to those whom he loves. I need to pray for prodigals, that they might return to a welcoming Father. For the prodigal world, too.

We now move from thinking out loud to prayer. The prayer doesn't need to use everything we've discovered; though if you have time, it can do. Again, as above, perhaps you'd like to reread the passage and what's been said here and form your own prayer. Use what's been said, but also write your own thoughts down, too.

Acts 4:23–31

On their release, Peter and John went back to their own people and reported all that the chief priests and the elders had said to them. When they heard this, they raised their voices together in prayer to God. 'Sovereign Lord,' they said, 'you made the heavens and the earth and the sea, and everything in them. You spoke by the Holy Spirit through the mouth of your servant, our father David:
> "Why do the nations rage
>   and the peoples plot in vain?
> The kings of the earth rise up
> and the rulers band together
>   against the Lord
>   and against his anointed one."

Indeed Herod and Pontius Pilate met together with the Gentiles and the people of Israel in this city to conspire against your holy servant Jesus, whom you anointed. They did what your power and will had decided beforehand should happen. Now, Lord, consider their threats and enable your servants to speak your word with great boldness. Stretch out your hand to heal and perform signs and wonders through the name of your holy servant Jesus.'

After they prayed, the place where they were meeting was shaken. And they were all filled with the Holy Spirit and spoke the word of God boldly.

Thinking out loud

As we did when we looked at 2 Chronicles 30:23–27 above, this is a passage for which we could choose a title that seems to cover its purpose. In this case, perhaps, 'Answered prayer' or 'Godly praying'.

In this chapter of Acts, Luke writes about a church in imminent danger. The previous verses have seen Peter and John called before the powerful Sanhedrin because they had healed a crippled man in the name of Jesus Christ. Instead of rejoicing in the power and goodness of God, as they should have, the Jewish leaders threatened the apostles not to preach or to teach in that name and sent them away—hence the phrase, 'On their release' (v. 23). In this short passage the apostles return to the fellowship of believers, recounting their story. This is followed by immediate, bold and fervent prayer.

I notice, first, that their prayer in a difficult situation begins with a reminder and an affirmation of the God to whom they pray: 'Sovereign Lord, you made the heavens and the earth and the sea, and everything in them' (v. 24). Their prayer starts with the thought of who God is, not with the difficult situation they face, however trying that is and however fearful that makes them feel. God is the sovereign Lord, a ruler of unchallengeable power. He's the creator of everything that exists. There's no one equal to him. Faced with daunting circumstances, the church reminds itself that God, to whom they pray, is greater than anything they face.

The prayer then turns to remember that God is the one who speaks, the God of revelation and truth, the God interested and involved enough to address his people and the God of history—specifically, covenant history with the mention of their 'father', David (vv. 25–26). Then, quoting a wonderful royal psalm attributed to David and reinterpreting it as a psalm about the Messiah, they apply the powerful words to the situation in which Jesus was taken, humiliated and executed on the cross. At first sight, this seems to me strange encouragement. But apparently the Lord had it all planned: 'They did what your power and will had decided beforehand should happen' (v. 28). So, what looked like failure was in the divine purpose. (This may be a theological thought that you might like to leave until another time, like the barn in the Holman Hunt illustration earlier. It opens up a whole host of themes like providence, sovereignty, free will, and so on. For this exercise, at this point, just state it in faith and move on.)

Finally, at verse 29 the church petitions God. Only after worshipping the Lord, acknowledging who he is and reminding themselves of his powerful ability and purpose does the church ask anything. They ask three things: that God considers 'their threats' (that is, that he bears them in mind), that he enables his servants to speak boldly (v. 29) and that he acts on their behalf authenticating that message by revealing his love and power in the world in healing, signs and wonders (v. 30); spiritual gifts and miracles.

It seems to me that the disciples' prayer acknowledges their own inadequacy and the divine sufficiency. And, recognising this, they put the whole situation into the hands of God. And look what happens: 'After they prayed, the place where they were meeting was shaken. And they were all filled with the Holy Spirit and spoke the word of God boldly' (v. 31). God is tangibly present among them. The Holy Spirit of God emboldens them to preach the good news of Christ to a waiting world—the Lord is revered and glorified.

From our thinking out loud on the passage, we might now move to the four strands of Martin Luther's prayer garland: instruction, thanksgiving/praise, confession and supplication.

1 Instruction or teaching: What is the Lord seeking to teach me from this passage? What do I need to know?

In the face of considerable threat to the church's and their own personal well-being and lives, the response of the fellowship is not to consider their own gifts or courage, but to turn unreservedly to God, who they know to be equal to the task. In confidence they say that they know he is all-powerful, creator of all things, ruler of history itself, saviour and sustainer of his people. They say, in effect, 'It is to you we turn. Who else could we turn to? Our hope is in you. You are all we need at this time, in this hour. Our faith looks to you.' It seems to me that they do this because their prayer reflects their faith; their prayer is an expression of their spiritual life. Seeing God as he is put prayer at the centre of their response to the situation they found themselves in. Conversely, praying put the Lord at the centre of their situation. My faith should be reflected in my praying, too.

2 Thanksgiving or praise: What should I be grateful for on reading this portion of scripture?

I praise God for the God he is revealed to be in this short passage. He stands above all of the difficult situations I face, but he's also intimately involved in them. He's a God of power and goodness. His purpose is to bless the world through Jesus Christ, even when the world rejects him.

I'm grateful, too, that in difficult and troubling circumstances in which I've been involved, the Lord has always been there in grace. He's answered prayer, sometimes in remarkable ways. He's authenticated his word. He's grown his church.

It's now your turn to have a go at the final two strands of Luther's garland: confession and prayer/supplication. It might help at this stage to use what I've said above, but you don't have to, of course.

3 Confession or repentance

How does this passage impinge on my conscience and what in it encourages me to confess particular sins? What sins shall I confess?

4 Prayer or supplication

What do I now need to pray for, to cry out to God for?

We now move from thinking out loud to prayer. The prayer doesn't need to use everything we've discovered; though if you have time, it can do. Reread the passage and what's been said here and form your own prayer. Use what's been said, but also write your own thoughts down, too.

Galatians 5:1–13

It is for freedom that Christ has set us free. Stand firm, then, and do not let yourselves be burdened again by a yoke of slavery. Mark my words! I, Paul, tell you that if you let yourselves be circumcised, Christ will be of no value to you at all. Again I declare to every man who lets himself be circumcised that he is required to obey the whole law. You who are trying to be justified by the law have been alienated from Christ; you have fallen away from grace. For through the Spirit we eagerly await by faith the righteousness for which we hope. For in Christ Jesus neither circumcision nor uncircumcision has any value. The only thing that counts is faith expressing itself through love.

You were running a good race. Who cut in on you to keep you from obeying the truth? That kind of persuasion does not come from the one who calls you. 'A little yeast works through the whole batch of dough.' I am confident in the Lord that you will take no other view. The one who is throwing you into confusion, whoever that may be, will have to pay the penalty. Brothers and sisters, if I am still preaching circumcision, why am I still being persecuted? In that case the offence of the cross has been abolished. As for those agitators, I wish they would go the whole way and emasculate themselves!

You, my brothers and sisters, were called to be free. But do not use your freedom to indulge the flesh; rather, serve one another humbly in love.

Thinking out loud

Sometimes a passage will have a clear topic sentence (remember those at school?), and the first sentence in this text is definitely one. Everything else that the apostle Paul says seems to hang from it, to qualify it, to enlarge upon it. If we discern a topic sentence, the shape of the passage and its meaning should become clear.

What a terrific passage of scripture. Here's a radical idea that, if I'm honest, I know I find difficult to grasp: if I am a Christian, I am free. I know that in saying it I immediately start to qualify the statement with a number of 'ifs' and 'buts'. However, Paul appears to mean that I am *really* free. No qualifying points. I am really *free*.[25] The freedom that Paul speaks of is a gift from the Son of God. He says, 'Christ has set us free.' That's the *radical* nature of being a child of God.

I notice how Galatians 5 begins with such a bold statement: 'For freedom Christ has set us free.' I want to shout the sentence as I read it out loud to myself. (That sometimes helps, by the way.) This appears to be a passionate cry from the apostle's heart. There is an abruptness about the exclamation: 'For freedom Christ has set us free.' It comes across as a sort of slogan or a banner. I have preached in little churches where the ten commandments were on plaques on the wall, intimidating both the congregation and the preacher; the congregation has them ever before them, the preacher has them to their back. Perhaps Paul would have taken these down, and painted in huge, bright, colourful letters this slogan instead: 'It is for freedom that Christ has set us free.'

For the apostle, freedom appears to characterise the gospel from beginning to end. It's important too that Paul doesn't appeal to his readers to fight to be free. Later, Luther would have also assured us that we have not been liberated by our own efforts; we're simply unable to do so. It is a freedom given us by Christ; it is the goal of the divine act of redemption. The Lord has sought us and taken us from being captive and has set us free.

It reminds me of Wesley's great hymn, which picks up something of this imagery:

Long my imprisoned spirit lay
Fast bound in sin and nature's night;
Thine eye diffused a quickening ray
I woke, the dungeon flamed with light.
My chains fell off, my heart was free;
I rose, went forth, and followed thee.
Charles Wesley, 1707–88

My own coming to Christ could have been described in such imagery, too. The apostle goes on, 'do not let yourselves be burdened again' (v. 1). I can almost see Paul grabbing these Christians (and me) by the shoulders and shaking us (see Galatians 3:1). How easily I try to maintain my relationship with God by my own 'works'—just like them.

They were doing well: 'You were running a good race,' Paul says (v. 7). They had clearly believed in Christ for salvation; but perhaps they felt that they could only be sure of God's acceptance and approval by taking that final step of belonging to the circumcised. The apostle is astounded by this. Christ came to give freedom from all of this. If you're free in Christ there can be no compulsion to be burdened again with the crushing weight of nationalism, custom, obligation, law (see Galatians 3:28).

Paul is adamant about this and uses very strong language to persuade the Galatians. 'If you let yourselves be circumcised, Christ will be of no value to you at all' (v. 2). The approval of God comes solely through my identification and living relationship with Jesus Christ. That is sufficient. There is need for nothing else to gain divine approval or to be sure of God's approval. Jesus is everything. To put it another way: If I don't trust *only* in Christ for salvation, then Christ is of no value whatever to me.

'Again I declare to every man who lets himself be circumcised that he is required to obey the whole law' (v. 3). Paul recognises the logic of what is going on. It appears that what they demanded was not the single act of circumcision, but the whole way of life that went with it. Circumcision was the first act of full covenant membership and obligation. It was to adopt a Jewish way of life. Yet Paul is arguing that Christ has fulfilled the law for us and has become a curse for us that we might be free.

'You who are trying to be justified by law have been alienated from Christ; you have fallen away from grace' (v. 4). That's a pretty powerful verse. In presently trying to live righteously by law, they have *already* let go of Christ! (Here's a 'barn' which I'm going to leave until tomorrow: Are we able to fall from divine grace? Or is this rhetorical in the apostle's argument?)[26]

I'm left with the conclusion that to be free as a Christian is to accept the salvation and the approval of God on the basis of Christ alone. In other words, this is the way God means it to be accepted—as a gift. This is a radical biblical idea for me to grasp. On the other hand, the passage indicates that being a slave, as opposed to being free in Christ, on one level at least, is to seek to find continued acceptance with God by something other than the free grace of God in Christ. It is to live life in a way that is contrary to that for which Christ freed us. It is to allow something or someone other than the Lord Jesus Christ and his Spirit to be determinative of the way I live. It is to be distracted from the truth of the gospel—that is, the centrality and all-sufficiency of Jesus Christ for salvation and for the daily experience of knowing that God loves me.

From my thinking out loud on the passage, we might now move to the four strands of Martin Luther's prayer garland: instruction, thanksgiving/praise, confession and supplication.

1 **Instruction or teaching**: What is the Lord seeking to teach me from this passage? What do I need to know?

There are at least two areas in which this passage speaks powerfully to me. First, I think of times I've been legalistic, perhaps. For example, I know that I sometimes try to make up for things if I do something wrong. I imagine being on a diet but starting the day with a slice of chocolate cake: that's 27 points, straight away! All day afterwards, I'd be trying to avoid food to make up for the early morning mistake. I know I'm a bit like that in my spiritual life. If I make a mistake (sin—let's call it what it is), I try harder for a good while afterwards in order somehow to make up for it; in order to make sure my relationship with God is on the right track; that he still loves me, even though I sinned. What Paul is reminding me here very forcefully is that my relationship with God—both its instigation and its continuance—comes from grace, from what Jesus Christ has done for me. It doesn't come from me. It doesn't come from what I have or can do. My goodness didn't forge my relationship with God. My trying (Luther spoke of 'works') won't maintain that relationship. It comes through Jesus Christ alone. By thinking (even subconsciously) that I'm accepted by God because I somehow deserve it, I lessen the value of Christ in the whole dynamic and process of my salvation. This is dishonouring to God. Paul says that I have been freed from all that.

A second area in which I seem to follow the Galatians is related to past sin and failure. I sometimes feel enslaved by this; almost paralysed.[27] God measures my future by what Jesus has accomplished, not by my spotless (or not) past. My usefulness to him and to his kingdom is dependent on the divine love in Christ, not on my achievement. Again, the apostle Paul tells me to be free as Christ has made me free.

2 **Thanksgiving or praise**: What should I be grateful for on reading this portion of scripture?

I am grateful to God for loving me in Jesus Christ; in making him central and sufficient for my salvation; in making me truly free in him. I'm grateful that my salvation is accomplished through grace in Christ's life and death. I need add nothing to it; indeed, I cannot!

As above, it's now your turn to have a go at the final two strands of Luther's garland: confession and prayer/supplication. It might help at this stage to use what I've said above, but you don't have to, of course.

3 Confession or repentance

How does this passage impinge on my conscience and what in it encourages me to confess particular sins? What sins shall I confess?

4 Prayer or supplication

What do I now need to pray for, to cry out to God for?

We now move from thinking out loud to prayer. The prayer doesn't need to use everything we've discovered; though if you have time, it can do. Again, as above, perhaps you'd like to reread the passage and what's been said here and form your own prayer. Use what's been said, but also write your own thoughts down, too.

Colossians 3:4–10

When Christ, who is your life, appears, then you also will appear with him in glory. Put to death, therefore, whatever belongs to your earthly nature: sexual immorality, impurity, lust, evil desires and greed, which is idolatry. Because of these, the wrath of God is coming. You used to walk in these ways, in the life you once lived. But now you must also rid yourselves of all such things as these: anger, rage, malice, slander, and filthy language from your lips. Do not lie to each other, since you have taken off your old self with its practices and have put on the new self, which is being renewed in knowledge in the image of its Creator.

Thinking out loud

Again, as we've discovered above, it's sometimes good to discern a shape to the passage, especially if that shape is repeated elsewhere in scripture. This is the case with this passage from the apostle's letter to the Colossian church. Let me explain this shape—it will help here and in future exercises.

Let me begin with an illustration. I used to teach. I did so for a good number of years—mostly very enjoyably. I remember that when I was a Head of House in a large, challenging comprehensive school, I used to try to encourage good behaviour by reminding pupils what was expected. So, traditionally, at the first assembly of the academic year I would look hundreds of lively and inquisitive youngsters in the eyes and say that because they were in Denman House I would expect good behaviour from them. I must say, thankfully, most children were well behaved anyway, and those who weren't were not going to be fooled by such an optimistic greeting. But, generally, it made me feel better all the same; I felt I'd done my bit. What I was trying to do was to say that because they were such and such, therefore they would behave in a certain way. The formal terms for these two parts are indicative and imperative. The indicative tells us who we are; the imperative tells us what to do. The indicative somehow defines us; the imperative is the active consequence of that. The indicative is a statement; the imperative is a command. The indicative in this illustration is that they are members of my house, Denman House. That's where they belong, that's who they are, and that defines them (in that limited context of school, at least). The imperative in the illustration is the demand that they behave in a certain way; that is, that they behave well. The indicative and imperative often work together with a 'therefore' between: 'You are in Denman House, therefore you will behave like this.' (See verse 5 above for a clear example of this.)

Paul often uses this same distinction and shape. And, it's a really important one.[28] Here in Colossians 3 he does this quite clearly. He uses two indicatives and follows these with two resulting imperatives. Indicative 1: 'When Christ, who is your life, appears, then you also will appear with him in glory' (v. 4). Wow! Indicative 2: 'you have taken off your old self … [you] have put on the new self, which is being renewed in knowledge in the image of its Creator' (vv. 9 and 10). In a sense, these indicatives define the recipients. Indicatives are statements. The second one says something about them today, in the present: they are new. The first indicative says something about their future: they will be with Christ in glory. Imperatives, on the other hand, are demands. On the basis of these two amazing and defining truths, the apostle demands from them behaviour that reflects that reality: 'sexual immorality, impurity, lust, evil desires and greed' … 'anger, rage, malice, slander, filthy language' and lying (vv. 5, 8–9) are to be things of the past. Here is the truth of the matter, says Paul: now live accordingly. Because of that truth, says Paul, they need to 'put to death' (v. 5) or 'rid' themselves (v. 8) of old ways, old attitudes and old habits. They are simply no longer appropriate. The indicatives (the new self, a glorious future with Christ) necessitate the imperatives (putting to death, ridding themselves). Who I am in Christ should (must) determine my behaviour.

Now, of course, there's a very significant difference between me telling students they belong and therefore that they should behave well and the apostle Paul telling us. I had no means at all to empower the pupils to better behaviour. However, elsewhere, Paul assures us of the empowering and sanctifying presence of the Holy Spirit in our lives (see Romans 8:1–17 and Galatians 5:16–26, for example). Here, in Colossians, he simply assures us that Christ is our life. Everything we need we have in him.

From our thinking out loud on the passage, we might now move to the four strands of Martin Luther's prayer garland: instruction, thanksgiving/praise, confession and supplication.

1 Instruction or teaching: What is the Lord seeking to teach me from this passage? What do I need to know?

I need to grasp this again: that the indicative necessitates the imperative. This is a fascinating connection. But, if it is true, it needs to be more than simply fascinating. I need to spend more time and energy working on understanding the truths of the faith, the doctrines of scripture, because it is when I grasp those that I'll be able better to live a life worthy of my salvation, of God and of Jesus Christ. Paul's instructions are not simply pragmatic. They don't come from nowhere. They are rooted in truth, the reality of my situation in Christ.

2 Thanksgiving or praise: What should I be grateful for on reading this portion of scripture?

I'm grateful for the amazing truth that I have a future that is somehow caught up in the glorious appearance of Jesus Christ. Until then, I'm being renewed (present continuous) 'in knowledge in the image of its Creator' (v. 10). I'm thankful because that continuous renewal suggests that I haven't yet made it, that I'm a work still in progress; but that God is still working on me and with me, to his glory.

As above, it's now your turn to have a go at the final two strands of Luther's garland: confession and prayer/supplication. It might help at this stage to use what I've said above, but you don't have to, of course.

3 Confession or repentance

How does this passage impinge on my conscience and what in it encourages me to confess particular sins? What sins shall I confess?

4 Prayer or supplication

What do I now need to pray for, to cry out to God for?

We now move from thinking out loud to prayer. The prayer doesn't need to use everything we've discovered; though if you have time, it can do. Again, as above, perhaps you'd like to reread the passage and what's been said here and form your own prayer. Use what's been said, but also write your own thoughts down, too.

1 John 3:1–3

See what great love the Father has lavished on us, that we should be called children of God! And that is what we are! The reason the world does not know us is that it did not know him. Dear friends, now we are children of God, and what we will be has not yet been made known. But we know that when Christ appears, we shall be like him, for we shall see him as he is. All who have this hope in him purify themselves, just as he is pure.

Thinking out loud

What is the subject of this short passage? If we work that out the rest will follow.

This short passage is about the relationship that I have with God, and the miracle of it. He is my Father, I'm his child. And John wants to underline that and to affirm it in the strongest way: 'And that is what we are!' he says (v. 1). Again, in verse 2, 'now we are children of God'. That is what I am: his child, God's child. Amazing! The apostle stresses the fact that I am a child simply because of the generous love of God, which is extravagant; he lavishes it on us. Elsewhere in the New Testament, Paul speaks about God adopting us and John is saying something similar here. It is the love of God poured out on us that causes us to be his children. We're entitled to that status simply because of divine grace.

Our being children of God is clear. We live in that relationship and that experience day by day. However, there is also mystery involved in our adoption as children of God. There is still a great deal to be revealed. John states that 'what we will be has not yet been made known' (v. 2). We're assured of the present, gracious reality. But what does this entail, and what does this look like in the spiritual reality of the new heavens and the new earth, on Christ's return? We can't even guess, but we are told here that, remarkably, 'when Christ appears, we shall be like him, for we shall see him as he is' (v. 2). When I read this I'm staggered by the teaching that I will somehow be like Jesus Christ, that seeing him will mark the juncture between what I am now and what I will be in eternity. That gives me hope. I won't always be the sinful and fallen man I am today. I won't always be struggling as I am today. I will be changed. I will be like him whom I love.

That hope, says John, is enough to encourage me to 'purify' myself (v. 3), to spur myself on to be as much like Jesus as I can be, even in my human fragility and fallenness. If I'm going to be like Jesus one day in the future (and into eternity, of course), then I want to be like him today and tomorrow, in the concreteness of my daily being and living. Jesus Christ is pure (v. 3), I want to be pure—even if the world doesn't understand me; after all, it clearly didn't understand him (v. 1).

From our thinking out loud on the passage, we might now move to the four strands of Martin Luther's prayer garland: instruction, thanksgiving/praise, confession and supplication.

1 Instruction or teaching: What is the Lord seeking to teach me from this passage? What do I need to know?

The Lord teaches me that I am a child of God: adopted, loved and kept by grace alone. He has saved me and taken me into his family. I have a status—as do all of his children. We are children of the living God, children of the King. This is a reality now and will continue into and throughout eternity. It is the contrast between the purity of the future and the imperfections of the present that gives me hope and that motivates me to godliness today.

2 Thanksgiving or praise: What should I be grateful for on reading this portion of scripture?

I am so grateful for the love of God that sees me in Christ and adopts me as a child. What grace, what love lavished upon me!

It's now your turn to have a go at the final two strands of Luther's garland: confession and prayer/supplication. It might help at this stage to use what I've said above, but you don't have to, of course.

3 Confession or repentance

How does this passage impinge on my conscience and what in it encourages me to confess particular sins? What sins shall I confess?

4 Prayer or supplication

What do I now need to pray for, to cry out to God for?

We now move from thinking out loud to prayer. The prayer doesn't need to use everything we've discovered; though if you have time, it can do. Again, as above, perhaps you'd like to reread the passage and what's been said here and form your own prayer. Use what's been said, but also write your own thoughts down, too.

I think you may well have grasped the idea of Luther's pattern of praying by now, what he called his fourfold garland. I hope you see its usefulness, though you may see this more if you have a go yourself, without much input from me. The next chapter gives you that chance.

Chapter 5

Following Luther's example: going solo

In this chapter I basically leave you to have a go yourself. If you found my reflections and prayers helpful in the previous chapter, and I hope you did, follow my example as I followed Luther's. I recommend here passages of scripture to read and to reflect upon and I make a few suggestions that I hope will make the task a little easier at this stage. You can do with these comments what you like. But, apart from this minimal help, you're on your own from now on.

Before we begin, let's recall the four strands that form the method of Bible reading. They are:

- instruction, or teaching
- thanksgiving, or grateful praise
- confession, or repentance
- prayer, or supplication

Let's also keep in mind the questions that will allow and encourage you to apply these aspects to your own life and spiritual development as a follower of Jesus Christ. So ask:

- What is the Lord seeking to teach me from this passage? What do I need to know?
- What should I be grateful for on reading this portion of scripture?
- How does this passage impinge on my conscience and what in it encourages me to confess particular sins? What sins shall I confess?
- What do I now need to pray for, to cry out to God for?

Also, here is a reminder of the more pertinent items from the list of guidelines to help make your experience of praying more purposeful.

- Sit in a comfortable chair; preferably away from distractions
- Pray for God the Holy Spirit to help
- Stick to the task in hand
- Take the suggested questions seriously
- Keep God and Jesus as central, not self
- After reading and final prayer, wait on the Lord!

Numbers 6:22–27

The Lord said to Moses, 'Tell Aaron and his sons, "This is how you are to bless the Israelites. Say to them:
'The Lord will bless you
and keep you;
the Lord make his face shine on you
and be gracious to you;
the Lord turn his face towards you
and give you peace.'"
'So they will put my name on the Israelites, and I will bless them.'

Thinking out loud

This is quite clearly instruction about blessing. You might notice, perhaps, how the one blessing (God's presence) is phrased in different ways.

- The Lord desires to bless his people (v. 27)—what does that say about the Lord and his love for the Israelites (and for us)?
- Interestingly, he speaks about Aaron and his sons (v. 23), suggesting, perhaps, a future relationship as well as the current one.
- Blessing is an interesting subject.[29] It appears from this passage that to say a blessing *is* to bless. Moses, Aaron and his sons speak the divine blessing upon the people of Israel. It entails keeping them (v. 24), being gracious to them (v. 25), giving them peace (v. 26). What areas in your life and of others' need divine blessing spoken into them?

1 Instruction or teaching

What is the Lord seeking to teach me from this passage? What do I need to know?

2 Thanksgiving or praise

What should I be grateful for on reading this portion of scripture?

3 Confession or repentance

How does this passage impinge on my conscience and what in it encourages me to confess particular sins? What sins shall I confess?

4 Prayer or supplication

What do I now need to pray for, to cry out to God for?

A prayer

1 Kings 19:9–13

And the word of the Lord came to him: 'What are you doing here, Elijah?'

He replied, 'I have been very zealous for the Lord God Almighty. The Israelites have rejected your covenant, torn down your altars, and put your prophets to death with the sword. I am the only one left, and now they are trying to kill me too.'

The Lord said, 'Go out and stand on the mountain in the presence of the Lord, for the Lord is about to pass by.'

Then a great and powerful wind tore the mountains apart and shattered the rocks before the Lord, but the Lord was not in the wind. After the wind there was an earthquake, but the Lord was not in the earthquake. After the earthquake came a fire, but the Lord was not in the fire. And after the fire came a gentle whisper. When Elijah heard it, he pulled his cloak over his face and went out and stood at the mouth of the cave.

Then a voice said to him, 'What are you doing here, Elijah?'

Thinking out loud

Here, you might like to look at the two characters involved in the narrative. And also the repeated question, 'What are you doing here, Elijah?' (vv. 9 and 13).

- The Lord twice asks Elijah what he is doing there. The question certainly indicates geographical position; might it imply something else too? What?
- Elijah is sorry for himself: he's been zealous, rejected, isolated and now afraid (v. 10).
- What he needs is the presence of the Lord (v. 11). The Lord knows this.

- The wind, earthquake and fire came as powerful experiences. The Lord *could* have been in them, but wasn't. Why does God let the prophet experience these somewhat empty signs at this time?
- The whisper is gentle—the Lord *is* in this. But he asks the same question: 'What are you doing here, Elijah?' (v. 13). What might be the significance of the gentle whisper following the powerful signs experienced earlier? What is the point for us?

1 Instruction or teaching

What is the Lord seeking to teach me from this passage? What do I need to know?

2 Thanksgiving or praise

What should I be grateful for on reading this portion of scripture?

3 Confession or repentance

How does this passage impinge on my conscience and what in it encourages me to confess particular sins? What sins shall I confess?

4 Prayer or supplication

What do I now need to pray for, to cry out to God for?

A prayer

Psalm 36:5–9

Your love, Lord, reaches to the heavens,
   your faithfulness to the skies.
Your righteousness is like the highest mountains,
   your justice like the great deep.
   You, Lord, preserve both people and animals.
How priceless is your unfailing love, O God!
   People take refuge in the shadow of your wings.
They feast in the abundance of your house;
   you give them drink from your river of delights.
For with you is the fountain of life;
   in your light we see light.

Thinking out loud

How do we speak to God of God? Are words adequate?

It's impossible to exaggerate when we speak of God. He is so magnificent that language is simply inadequate. We soon reach its limits as we try to worship him. Yet the psalmist attempts it anyway.

- God's love 'reaches to the heavens' (v. 5); it's 'priceless' (v. 7)
- God's faithfulness reaches 'to the skies'
- God's righteousness is 'like the highest mountains'
- God's justice is 'like the great deep'

These appear almost theoretical attributes until the psalmist applies them:

- God preserves both animals and human beings (v. 6)
- God protects people (v. 7)

- God is generous (v. 8)
- God is life and light (v. 9)

1 Instruction or teaching

What is the Lord seeking to teach me from this passage? What do I need to know?

2 Thanksgiving or praise

What should I be grateful for on reading this portion of scripture?

3 Confession or repentance

How does this passage impinge on my conscience and what in it encourages me to confess particular sins? What sins shall I confess?

4 Prayer or supplication

What do I now need to pray for, to cry out to God for?

A prayer

Psalm 42:1–5

As the deer pants for streams of water,
  so my soul pants for you, my God.
My soul thirsts for God, for the living God.
  When can I go and meet with God?
My tears have been my food
  day and night,
while people say to me all day long,
  'Where is your God?'
These things I remember
  as I pour out my soul
how I used to go to the house of God
  under the protection of the Mighty One
with shouts of joy and praise
  among the festive throng.
Why, my soul, are you downcast?
  Why so disturbed within me?
Put your hope in God,
  for I will yet praise him,
  my Saviour and my God.

Thinking out loud

There is movement and determination about the psalmist's attitude towards his circumstances.

Looking carefully at this well-known psalm we find that there are two basic problems that the psalmist faces: he lacks present experience of the living God (v. 2); he is being ridiculed about his faith (v. 3). This causes him to be downcast and disturbed, weeping day and night (v. 3).

Having considered this situation, and perhaps looking at times in your own experience when similar things have happened, it may help to ask what the psalmist does about his circumstances. Look at the verbs related to this:

- 'my soul *pants* for you' (v. 1)
- 'my soul *thirsts* for God' (v. 2)
- 'I *pour out* my soul' (v. 4)
- he *remembers* much better times (v. 4)
- he *hopes* in God (v. 5)
- he *recognises* God as his Saviour and his God (v. 5)

Perhaps you could work through this list and imagine what each might have meant for the psalmist. What do they mean to you today?

1 Instruction or teaching

What is the Lord seeking to teach me from this passage? What do I need to know?

2 Thanksgiving or praise

What should I be grateful for on reading this portion of scripture?

3 Confession or repentance

How does this passage impinge on my conscience and what in it encourages me to confess particular sins? What sins shall I confess?

4 Prayer or supplication

What do I now need to pray for, to cry out to God for?

A prayer

Isaiah 43:10–12

'You are my witnesses,' declares the Lord,
    'and my servant whom I have chosen,
so that you may know and believe me
    and understand that I am he.
Before me no god was formed,
    nor will there be one after me.
I, even I, am the Lord,
    and apart from me there is no saviour.
I have revealed and saved and proclaimed—
    I, and not some foreign god among you.
You are my witnesses,' declares the Lord, 'that I am God.'

Thinking out loud

Like the Elijah passage above, this text from Isaiah starts and finishes with the same words: 'You are my witnesses.' Does this shape help us to read and understand the passage?

Here is a declaration from God himself which defines the people of Israel: 'You are my witnesses' (v. 10; and again in v. 12—an important indicative of scripture). Its repetition shapes the passage; it underlines its importance—particularly as the second use indicates exactly what they are witnesses to; 'that I am God' (v. 12).

The calling of Israel to witness has as its foundation the fact that they have been chosen; their servanthood is determined by God's previous call. And he has chosen them to know, to believe and to understand that he is God (v. 10). Quite a calling, privilege and responsibility. Basically, they are to witness to divine revelation about himself and divine salvation: God's words and deeds. He emphasises this: 'I, even I, am the Lord, and apart from me there is no saviour' (v. 11). Notice, too, the verbs 'revealed', 'saved' and 'proclaimed'.

You might wrestle with what this meant for the Israelites, before turning your attention to what it means for the church today, and for you as an individual. How are we witnesses to the fact that God is who he says he is? What does that mean in our culture, in our particular lives?

1 Instruction or teaching

What is the Lord seeking to teach me from this passage? What do I need to know?

2 Thanksgiving or praise

What should I be grateful for on reading this portion of scripture?

3 Confession or repentance

How does this passage impinge on my conscience and what in it encourages me to confess particular sins? What sins shall I confess?

4 Prayer or supplication

What do I now need to pray for, to cry out to God for?

A prayer

Matthew 13:44–46

'The kingdom of heaven is like treasure hidden in a field. When a man found it, he hid it again, and then in his joy went and sold all he had and bought that field.

'Again, the kingdom of heaven is like a merchant looking for fine pearls. When he found one of great value, he went away and sold everything he had and bought it.'

Thinking out loud

Here, there is repetition—what is it saying? This example is very short—don't expect to say a great deal about it, but seek to apply it to your own circumstances.

Notice that the similarities are striking. Both short parables are about the kingdom of God or heaven. Both indicate that the kingdom of heaven is precious—like treasure, like a wonderful pearl. It is of great value. Both show that to gain the kingdom is a costly thing: the first man sells all he has; the second, similarly, sells everything. The first reveals the sheer joy of finding the kingdom. The second, following closely, implies it.

So, here are the words and ideas you might like to work with:

- kingdom of heaven
- its value
- the cost
- the joy

What are you going to do with these? How does each impinge on your own thinking and experience of receiving the kingdom in Christ? How are these (and other) ideas going to work towards prayer?

1 Instruction or teaching

What is the Lord seeking to teach me from this passage? What do I need to know?

2 Thanksgiving or praise

What should I be grateful for on reading this portion of scripture?

3 Confession or repentance

How does this passage impinge on my conscience and what in it encourages me to confess particular sins? What sins shall I confess?

4 Prayer or supplication

What do I now need to pray for, to cry out to God for?

A prayer

John 1:14

The Word became flesh and made his dwelling among us. We have seen his glory, the glory of the one and only Son, who came from the Father, full of grace and truth.

Thinking out loud

This single verse reveals so much. Though it's pretty familiar, how does it engage you today?

'Flesh' makes the whole thing very concrete, material. Eugene Peterson in THE MESSAGE underlines this: 'The Word became flesh and blood, and moved into the neighbourhood.'

- glory
- grace
- truth

Is this how you see Jesus?

1 Instruction or teaching

What is the Lord seeking to teach me from this passage? What do I need to know?

2 Thanksgiving or praise

What should I be grateful for on reading this portion of scripture?

3 Confession or repentance

How does this passage impinge on my conscience and what in it encourages me to confess particular sins? What sins shall I confess?

4 Prayer or supplication

What do I now need to pray for, to cry out to God for?

A prayer

Galatians 3:1–5

You foolish Galatians! Who has bewitched you? Before your very eyes Jesus Christ was clearly portrayed as crucified. I would like to learn just one thing from you: did you receive the Spirit by the works of the law, or by believing what you heard? Are you so foolish? After beginning by means of the Spirit, are you now trying to finish by means of the flesh? Have you experienced so much in vain—if it really was in vain? So again I ask, does God give you his Spirit and work miracles among you by the works of the law, or by believing what you heard?

Thinking out loud

So many rhetorical questions! What lies beneath them?

What's being contrasted or compared here? Why does the apostle think the Galatians are foolish? What is the importance of the Holy Spirit in their lives? In your life?

1 Instruction or teaching

What is the Lord seeking to teach me from this passage? What do I need to know?

2 Thanksgiving or praise

What should I be grateful for on reading this portion of scripture?

3 Confession or repentance

How does this passage impinge on my conscience and what in it encourages me to confess particular sins? What sins shall I confess?

4 Prayer or supplication

What do I now need to pray for, to cry out to God for?

A prayer

Ephesians 1:13-14

And you also were included in Christ when you heard the message of truth, the gospel of your salvation. When you believed, you were marked in him with a seal, the promised Holy Spirit, who is a deposit guaranteeing our inheritance until the redemption of those who are God's possession—to the praise of his glory.

Thinking out loud

There is a Trinitarian shape to the apostle's thinking here—notice the Father ('God'), the Son ('Christ') and the Holy Spirit are integrally involved in our salvation.

The shape that Paul creates here is important, isn't it? Notice the words 'included', 'believed', 'until the redemption of those'— implying beginning and end: it outlines in brief the Christian's life and experience of God.

1 Instruction or teaching

What is the Lord seeking to teach me from this passage? What do I need to know?

2 Thanksgiving or praise

What should I be grateful for on reading this portion of scripture?

3 Confession or repentance

How does this passage impinge on my conscience and what in it encourages me to confess particular sins? What sins shall I confess?

4 Prayer or supplication

What do I now need to pray for, to cry out to God for?

A prayer

1 Thessalonians 5:16–24

Rejoice always, pray continually, give thanks in all circumstances; for this is God's will for you in Christ Jesus.

Do not quench the Spirit. Do not treat prophecies with contempt but test them all; hold on to what is good, reject every kind of evil.

May God himself, the God of peace, sanctify you through and through. May your whole spirit, soul and body be kept blameless at the coming of our Lord Jesus Christ. The one who calls you is faithful, and he will do it.

Thinking out loud

Remember indicatives and imperatives earlier? The imperatives (demands) are clear in this passage; what are the indicatives (statements)—explicit or implied?

1 Instruction or teaching

What is the Lord seeking to teach me from this passage? What do I need to know?

2 Thanksgiving or praise

What should I be grateful for on reading this portion of scripture?

3 Confession or repentance

How does this passage impinge on my conscience and what in it encourages me to confess particular sins? What sins shall I confess?

4 Prayer or supplication

What do I now need to pray for, to cry out to God for?

A prayer

Chapter 6

Following Luther's example: taking it further

Now, you take over almost entirely. As always, it would be good to remember the four strands that form Luther's method of Bible reading. They are:

- instruction, or teaching
- thanksgiving, or grateful praise
- confession, or repentance
- prayer, or supplication

Then, it will be helpful to keep in mind the questions that will allow and encourage you to apply these aspects to your own life and spiritual development as a follower of Jesus Christ. So you might ask:

- What is the Lord seeking to teach me from this passage? What do I need to know?
- What should I be grateful for on reading this portion of scripture?
- How does this passage impinge on my conscience and what in it encourages me to confess particular sins? What sins shall I confess?
- What do I now need to pray for, to cry out to God for?

Also, here is a reminder of the more pertinent items from the list of guidelines to help make your experience of praying more purposeful.

- Sit in a comfortable chair
- Pray for God to help
- Stick to the task in hand
- Take the suggested questions seriously

- Keep God and Jesus as central, not self
- After reading and prayer, wait on the Lord

Here, then, is a short list of passages that might be a good place to start. Again, they come from different genres of the Bible: history, poetry, prophecy, Gospel, letter. Remember that you might gain more from some passages than from others; some may take longer; some may be more significant for you at this time. Rest in the Spirit's work as he reveals things from scripture.

- Genesis 28:10–17
- Leviticus 20:7
- Psalm 23
- Psalm 100
- Isaiah 57:15–16
- Zechariah 2:10–11
- Matthew 7:7–12
- John 8:34–36
- Acts 3:1–10
- 2 Thessalonians 2:13–17
- Hebrews 10:19–25
- 1 Peter 1:8–9
- Revelation 3:7–13

There are three other possibilities that you might like to consider. First, you might like to take your favourite passages of the Bible and use those. In this way you'd be able to bring to bear your own past experience of the passage too. But, try hard not to be too tied to past experience. Second, if you know what the preacher is speaking on this weekend at church, look at that passage and see what you can glean from it before listening on Sunday. This can be a useful way of praying Luther's method and a very engaged way of listening to the sermon.

Third, something else to try, if you have the stamina, is to use the reformer's method through a whole book of the Bible. Why not start with a shorter one, or one that has clear shape to it; for example, Paul's letter to the Philippians. Try the following suggestions. I've attached 'headings' to the section breaks,[30] but you don't need to be ruled by them; they are there merely as focus pointers. The following could take you through three weeks; so, not terribly arduous, if you want to have a go.

Philippians

1:1-2	Paul's greeting
1:3-8	Paul remembers the believers
1:9-11	Paul's prayer
1:12-18	Paul's rejoicing, even through suffering
1:19-26	Paul and Jesus Christ
1:27-30	Life worthy of the gospel
2:1-5	Living together
2:5-11	Jesus' example
2:12-18	Working out our salvation
2:19-29	Respect for those ministering the gospel
3:1-6	Natural confidence
3:7-11	Confidence in Christ
3:12-14	Pressing on in faith
3:15-21	Hope through waiting
4:1-3	Standing firm in Christ
4:4-7	Faithful prayer
4:8-9	Think on good things
4:10-13	Godly contentment
4:14-20	Spiritual giving
4:21-23	Greetings and the grace of Jesus

Finally, why not plan to pray using Luther's method with someone else—a friend, a mentor, members of your home group, preaching or leadership teams? Apart from cementing relationships, this can be an exciting, purposeful and helpful way of reading scripture and praying together.

Chapter 7

Final thoughts

If you've got this far, including doing the exercises, well done! Would you allow me just a few final thoughts to conclude our journey? You might remember that we began this book by commenting on Eugene Peterson's assertion that prayer, being a dangerous occupation, should not be too lightly entered into. We illustrated this by looking at Martin Luther's experience in serving the Eucharist when he suddenly realised the 'danger' of speaking words to the living God and his ensuing struggle to find a gracious God and Father, through Jesus Christ. On the one hand, Peterson is adamant that prayer should be rooted in the word of God, the Bible, in which it finds its life and sustenance. And, on the other hand, the reformer found that a good reading of scripture would release him into the freedom of the children of God, including, importantly, a freedom to pray aright.

In looking at Luther's little book, *A Simple Way to Pray*, we discovered in Chapter 2 that he underlines several characteristics of prayer. Among them we might repeat and underline the following in particular. First, Luther encourages us to pray in a focused and intentional manner. Using his method of prayer, I hope you've discovered the benefit of this intentionality. As I said at the beginning, we don't need to use this method every time we pray, nor for long periods of time, but it is definitely helpful to set aside some days or weeks to focus on the word of God and to pray through it. It enables us to seek God in a way that takes up the whole of our attention, not just a fleeting thought, or a passing comment.

Second, Luther encourages us to read scripture to encourage prayer and to warm our hearts towards God. Prayer is rooted in scripture. It finds its life in the words already spoken by God. So, praying after thoughtfully reading and reflecting on a passage of scripture allows space for the inspiring work of the Holy Spirit. It is he who takes the words of the biblical passage and applies them to our hearts and lives. It is he who centres our thinking on the Lord Jesus Christ, who we find in scripture presented to us as our salvation. Indeed, we saw that Luther states that, in Jesus Christ, we already have everything. He alone is the basis by which we approach such a God in prayer and worship.

Third, we need to be confident that the Lord has heard our prayers. It is, as it were, as if we say our 'Amen' and God himself repeats *his* 'Amen' in affirmation of his purposes for us in Christ. We can be sure of this, says Luther. More sure, of course, if our prayers grow from our engagement with and grasp of his word.

Fourth and lastly, Luther speaks of the context of our praying. We need to remember that the context of our praying is as wide as the universal and eternal church itself. We saw that he sometimes goes into a room alone to pray, and at other times he joins the church congregated in the building down the road. But, he insists, the context is a good deal wider than that. When we pray, we do so in the worshipping and praying company of those everywhere in the world who call on the name of Jesus Christ and also in the company of those who have gone before us and worship at the throne of God even now. The Bible repeatedly gives us that context, whether it is in the stories of faithful men and women of the Old and New Testament narrative, or in its tantalising glimpses into heaven and to glory.

So, given Martin Luther's teaching on prayer and your own experience of praying the Bible through the four stranded garland of instruction, thanksgiving, confession and prayer, it might be good to reflect on your experience.

- Do you find the close association of Bible and prayer that both Luther and Peterson suggest helpful to praying? In what ways does it help? Are there things about it that hinder prayer, perhaps?

- Is there a particular biblical genre (history, prophecy, poetry, wisdom, Gospel, epistle, and so on) that you find easier to pray through? Why do you think that is?
- Has praying in Luther's way 'improved' your prayers or your Bible reading? (By 'improved', I'm asking whether you're more satisfied with your own prayer and Bible reading now than you were.)
- Does reading and reflecting on scripture before praying give you more confidence in approaching God? If so, why do you think that is?

Notes

1 Eugene Peterson, *Working the Angles: The shape of pastoral integrity* (Eerdmans, 1987), p. 30. See pp. 30–43 on praying the Bible.
2 Peterson, *Working the Angles*, p. 30, original emphasis.
3 Peterson, *Working the Angles*, p. 30.
4 Peterson, *Working the Angles*, p. 31.
5 Quoted in R. Bainton, *Here I Stand* (New York, 1950), p. 30.
6 Peterson, *Working the Angles*, p. 30, original emphasis.
7 Amazingly, perhaps, but understandably, the reformer credits the beginnings of the Reformation to his friend and counsellor Staupitz (*LW* 54.97). *LW* refers to *Luther's Works* (American edition) 55 volumes (Concordia/Fortress, 1955–86).
8 Luther wrote an important work on this subject, *On the Freedom of a Christian*, in 1520.
9 For what follows, see *LW* 43.193–211.
10 An idea so prevalent again in the contemporary church today. Luther's criticism here is valid, I think.
11 Romans 8:26–27 says, 'In the same way, the Spirit helps us in our weakness. We do not know what we ought to pray for, but the Spirit himself intercedes for us through wordless groans. And he who searches our hearts knows the mind of the Spirit, because the Spirit intercedes for God's people in accordance with the will of God.'
12 Later, Luther uses the same method on praying through the creed.
13 Luther appears only to have seen his first Bible in his early twenties; it was the Latin Vulgate version.
14 Mark Bradford, *Encountering the Risen Christ* (BRF, 2016), p. 17.
15 Bradford, *Encountering the Risen Christ*, p. 37.
16 I'm thinking here of an alternative reading of Psalm 22:3 that says, 'Yet you are holy, enthroned on the praises of Israel.'
17 See King David's similar difficulty in 2 Samuel 12.
18 This is a comment from the New Testament concerning Jesus Christ, of course. See Hebrews 13:8.
19 A reading of the whole of Lamentations shows clearly why there is this depth of sorrow.
20 Significantly, Paul speaks of spiritual life being given by God to those who were dead: 'But because of his great love for us, God, who is rich in mercy, made us alive with Christ even when we were dead in transgressions—it is by grace you are saved' (Ephesians 2:4–5).

21 As an aside, the important 20th-century theologian Karl Barth makes wonderful use of this parable in his theology in *Church Dogmatics*. Also, though a little dated, of course, Keith Green's evocative song 'The Prodigal Son Suite' is worth listening to.

22 It's not true freedom, just freedom as perceived by the son, as we will see.

23 We see that in effect when the father says to the other son, 'You are always with me and *everything I have* is yours' (Luke 15:31, emphasis added).

24 Philip Yancey, *What's So Amazing about Grace?* (Zondervan, 1997), p. 66.

25 It reminds me that Jesus himself said, 'If the Son sets you free, you will be free indeed' (John 8:36).

26 Paul's conclusion is a resounding statement in Galatians 5:6, 'For in Christ Jesus neither circumcision nor uncircumcision has any value. The only thing that counts is faith expressing itself through love.'

27 I remember a short illustration from Stephen Brown's wonderful book on grace called, *When Being Good Isn't Good Enough* (Lucid Books, 2014), p. 197. He is an American Presbyterian minister as well as an academic. He was once speaking with a man (presumably also a minister) who had made a massive mistake in his past and simply couldn't believe that God could forgive him. Stephen Brown encouraged him by speaking of God's love and grace and in saying that the Lord had a future for this man. But, and this has always interested me, as he was saying it he felt guilty because in his own heart he didn't know whether what the man had done had disqualified him from service. What he'd done must have been awful. Then Brown sensed the Lord's voice rebuking him: all he'd offered was time and a listening ear (in themselves good, of course), whereas the Lord had sent his Son to die for him. That shook me when I first read it. It still does.

28 For a longer explanation of this important subject, see Michael Parsons, 'Being Precedes Act: Indicative and imperative in Paul's writing' in B.S. Rosner (ed.), *Understanding Paul's Ethics: Twentieth century approaches* (Eerdmans, 1995), pp. 217–47.

29 See Russ Parker's fascinating short work on this, *Rediscovering the Ministry of Blessing* (SPCK, 2014). Chapter 3 concerns the Aaronic blessing.

30 Many of these come from the NIV subheadings for this book.

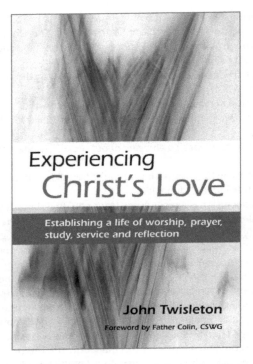

Experiencing
Christ's Love

Establishing a life of worship, prayer,
study, service and reflection

John Twisleton

Foreword by Father Colin, CSWG

In *Experiencing Christ's Love*, well-known writer John Twisleton reminds us of Jesus' gracious challenge to love God with heart, soul and mind, and to love our neighbour and ourselves. Against the backdrop of the message of God's unconditional love in Jesus Christ, the author delivers a wake-up call to the basic Christian patterns of worship, prayer, study, service and reflection. These, he claims, serve to take God's hand in ours, leading us into his divine possibilities.

Experiencing Christ's Love
Establishing a life of worship, prayer, study, service and reflection
John Twisleton
978 0 85746 517 7 £6.99

brfonline.org.uk

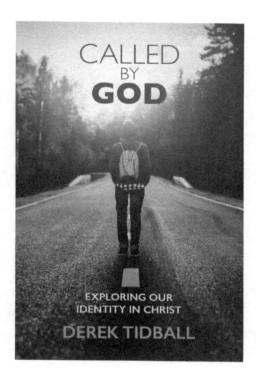

In an age in which it seems that everyone is concerned with their own identity, popular author and conference speaker Derek Tidball examines twelve key New Testament passages which go right to the heart of the matter. Identity for Christians, the Bible says, is rooted in who we are in Jesus Christ. Reflecting on Christian vocation, the author draws us back to see how the Bible speaks about the nature of who we have become by faith. Each chapter ends with questions, opening the reader to thoughtful and practical response.

Called by God
Exploring our identity in Christ
Derek Tidball
978 0 85746 530 6 £7.99

brfonline.org.uk

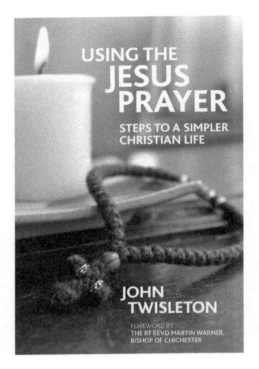

For over 15 centuries, repetition of the prayer 'Lord Jesus Christ, Son of God, have mercy on me, a sinner' has been an effective and practical way to cool the mind of anxiety and stress, enrich the spirit and more generally bring a restoring centring to life. Drawing on his own faith journey and pastoral experience, John Twisleton shares how use of the prayer brings a gift of simplicity that counters the postmodern fragmentation of Christian life.

Using the Jesus Prayer
Steps to a simpler Christian life
John Twisleton
978 0 84101 778 5 £6.99

brfonline.org.uk

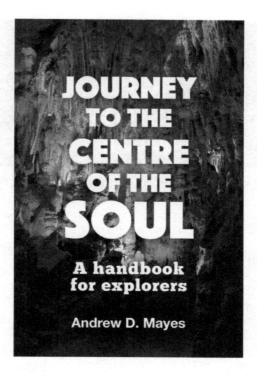

This unique and groundbreaking book is a summons to a subterranean spiritual adventure, an odyssey of the soul. If you let it, it will invigorate and inspire a search for something deeper in the spiritual life, and will link you with trusted spiritual guides to support you as you progress on a journey of discovery. *Journey to the Centre of the Soul* mines the rich seams of Christian spirituality, risks the depths, faces the darkness and makes astonishing, transformative discoveries.

Journey to the Centre of the Soul
Andrew D. Mayes
978 0 85746 582 5 £8.99

brfonline.org.uk

BRF

Transforming
lives and communities

Christian growth and understanding of the Bible

Resourcing individuals, groups and leaders in churches for their
own spiritual journey and for their ministry

Church outreach in the local community

Offering three programmes that churches are embracing
to great effect as they seek to engage
with their local communities
and transform lives

Teaching Christianity in primary schools

Working with children and teachers to explore Christianity
creatively and confidently

Children's and family ministry

Working with churches and families to explore Christianity
creatively and bring the Bible alive

Visit **brf.org.uk** for more information on BRF's work
Review this book on Twitter using **#BRFconnect**

brf.org.uk

The Bible Reading Fellowship (BRF) is a Registered Charity (No. 233280)